D1637435

POISON

AN ILLUSTRATED HISTORY

"What is there that is not a poison?
All substances are poisons,
there is none that is not a poison.
Only the dose determines that a
thing is not a poison."

Paracelsus (1493–1541)

POISON

AN ILLUSTRATED HISTORY

Joel Levy

LYONS PRESS
Guilford, Connecticut
An imprint of Globe Pequot Press

To buy books in quantity for corporate use
or incentives, call **(800) 962–0973**
or e-mail **premiums@GlobePequot.com**.

First published in the United States in 2011
by Lyons Press, an imprint of Globe Pequot
Press, by arrangement with Quid Publishing

9 8 7 6 5 4 3 2 1

Printed and bound in Malaysia for Imago

Library of Congress Cataloging-in-Publication
Data is available on file.

ISBN 978-0-7627-7056-4

Conceived, designed, and produced by

Quid Publishing
Level 4, Sheridan House,
114 Western Road,
Hove,
BN3 1DD
England

www.quidpublishing.com

Design by: Lindsey Johns

NOTE: The author, publisher, and copyright holder assume no responsibility
for any injury, loss, or damage caused or sustained as a consequence of the
use and application of the contents of this book.

This book details a wide range of extremely toxic substances. Any of them
can be lethal. None of the descriptions or explanations should be taken as
encouraging experimentation with or use of any toxic substance, or as a
substitute for medical care or expertise in responding to any exposure.
If you think you may have been exposed to a poisonous substance, seek
medical attention. And always bear in mind Lewis Carroll's admonition in
Alice's Adventures in Wonderland: "If you drink from a bottle marked
'poison,' it is almost certain to disagree with you sooner or later."

CONTENTS

Poison: An Introduction   6

Chapter One
Poison in Science   11

Chapter Two
Poison in Nature   37

Chapter Three
Poison in History   69

Chapter Four
Poison as Executioner   93

Chapter Five
Poison as Assassin   115

Chapter Six
Poison in Murder   143

Chapter Seven
Poison in Suicide   171

Chapter Eight
Poison as Savior   193

Acknowledgments   214

Glossary   215

References   219

Index   222

POISON: AN INTRODUCTION

The Greek myth of Jason and the Argonauts introduces the contradictory character of Medea, by turns a beautiful princess, forsaken bride, abominable child murderer, priestess, and witch. Above all, Medea is a brewer of potions, a poisoner. She drugs the serpent that guards the Golden Fleece; her potions heal the Argonaut Atalanta of her wounds, restore Jason's father Aeson to youth, and cleanse Hercules of his sin. She drives the bronze giant Talos insane with a psychoactive preparation; poisons a dress and crown to kill Jason's new bride, Glauce, and her father Creon; and attempts to destroy Theseus by lacing a cup of wine with deadly aconite, the poisonous herb that grew from the spittle of Cerberus, the hound of Hades.

All these disparate ends are achieved through the agency of magical herbs—substances of supernatural power, able to heal the sick, rejuvenate the old, strike down heroes, and twist the mind. In other words, substances that are as contradictory and mysterious as Medea herself, in whom are personified the many attributes of poison.

This book seeks to capture some of this complexity, to describe the manifold roles played by poison in history and culture, science and religion, medicine and murder. But it is first worth acknowledging that all poisons are simply chemicals. Their special status derives from the fact that they are pharmacologically potent—that's what makes them toxic, but it also gives them medicinal and intoxicant powers. Poison, medicine, intoxicant—all are facets of the same basic property.

Like Medea, poison can kill, drug, bewitch, or cure. And in the popular imagination it, too, has traditionally been associated with magic and myth—the world of witches and shamans. Even though more recent years have seen its reputation become less sacred and more profane—the province of murderers rather than magicians—poison is still mythologized and even romanticized. Poisons and poisoners still hold us in their thrall.

Medea and Jason by Florentine painter Girolamo Macchietti c.1570–5.

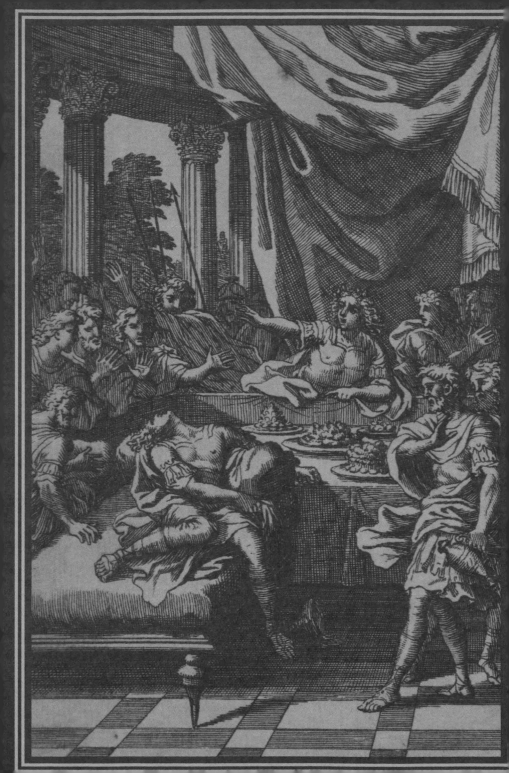

CHAPTER ONE

POISON

IN

SCIENCE

"What is there that is not a poison?"

Paracelsus (1493-1541)

NEARLY ALL BOOKS ABOUT POISON BEGIN WITH THE SAME QUOTE FROM SIXTEENTH-CENTURY PHYSICIAN AND NATURAL PHILOSOPHER PARACELSUS, A KEY FIGURE IN THE HISTORY OF POISONS. HIS OBSERVATIONS AND EXPERIENCE WITH BOTH POISONS AND MEDICINES LED PARACELSUS TO POSE AND ANSWER AN IMPORTANT QUESTION: "WHAT IS THERE THAT IS NOT A POISON? ALL SUBSTANCES ARE POISONS, THERE IS NONE THAT IS NOT A POISON. ONLY THE DOSE DETERMINES THAT A THING IS NOT A POISON."

This so-called "Paracelsus Principle" forms one of the basic tenets of toxicology and points to a fundamental truth about poisons—that they are chemicals, like all other substances. There is nothing magical or inherently sinister about a chemical that is poisonous; sometimes the same chemical in a smaller dose is harmless or even beneficial to health. To paraphrase Paracelsus: it is only the dose that determines whether a chemical is a poison.

For practical, legal, medical, and scientific purposes, however, the term "poison" tends to be more specifically defined, as something that is injurious to health even at low doses. This chapter explores definitions a little further, before moving on to the more important subject of how poisons get into the body and what happens to them once they're in. From here it explains how they affect the body at molecular, cellular, and physiological levels—the gruesome consequences of which recur throughout later chapters—and outlines the treatments and antidotes, if any, that are available to the victim.

What is a Poison?

A good place to start when seeking to understand poison is its technical definition as a substance that when taken into or absorbed by living organisms causes death or injury by means of its chemical action—especially such a material that is potent even in small doses. However, it is worth noting that legal definitions are often stricter, placing defined limits upon what is and what isn't a poison. For instance, in the U.S. a poison is legally defined as a substance that is lethal at doses of 50 mg per kg of body weight or less—for the average male this means less than 3.5 g, or about ¾ of a teaspoon.

However, such a specific definition is at odds with the more elastic nature of the term "poison" in wider usage. For example, an expert toxicologist is expected to know how to deal with thousands of chemicals with which people may come into contact; while, at the other extreme, the general public often limits its consideration of poisons to those sinister agents familiar from popular murder mysteries, such as arsenic and cyanide. In fact, as we shall see, both animals and assassins have made use of an extraordinary range of deadly chemicals, many of which we shall see within these pages, and all of which can truly be called poisons.

Competing Terms

There are many poison-related terms, of which "toxin" is perhaps the most important. This is the preferred term of scientists and clinicians but essentially carries the same meaning as "poison"—although it can also be used to refer solely to naturally occurring poisons. It derives from the Greek *toxikon*, meaning "arrow poison," an etymology that betrays the macabre relationship between people and poison throughout the ages.

The term "toxin" is most likely to be used when describing a specific chemical and, in turn, its specific actions in the body. For instance, a poison brewed from the opium poppy is likely to contain several different toxins, and a scientist would investigate the action of each of these toxins separately. Such a scientist would be called a toxicologist, toxicology being the study of toxins, and hence the science of poisons. Toxicology should, however, not be confused with toxicity, which refers to how toxic something is, and by extension the factors that determine this essential attribute.

Other terms that are also encountered in relation to poison include "contaminant," "pollutant," and "carcinogen." And while the terms "contaminant" and "pollutant" can both refer to poisons, they are more generally used in reference to substances that are toxic only at relatively high doses. Meanwhile, some poisons are indeed carcinogens—substances that cause cancer—but such carcinogenic effects are generally in addition to their primary toxic impact.

But enough of definitions for now. Let us turn instead to the terrible workings and fearful effects that poisons unleash once they have found their way, by fair means or foul, into the body.

The word *opium* derives from the Greek *opion* meaning "poppy juice," which reflects the method of obtaining sap by scratching a poppy's seed head. The active ingredients of this sap— among them morphine, codeine, thebaine, and papaverine—are collectively termed *opiates* and themselves reflect the varied nature of poisons. Morphine, for example, is one of the best painkillers in medicine, and heroin, though notorious as a highly addictive narcotic, is also a potent analgesic as diamorphine.

FIVE STEPS TO DEATH

How does a poison work? How can a single drop cause terrible illness, or even death? What makes one chemical deadly while another is harmless? To explain why poisons are poisonous it is necessary to look at the five stages that lead a chemical outside a healthy body to become a toxin inside a dead one: exposure, delivery, modification, action, and consequences.

Exposure

The route by which a poison gets into the body is crucial in determining its toxicity, how quickly it will act, which parts of the body it will affect, and what the victim's chances of survival are. And different modes of exposure can completely change whether a poison is deadly or harmless.

There are four main modes of exposure: via the digestive system—through the membranes of the digestive tract, the consequences of which may be affected by stomach acid and digestive enzymes; via the respiratory system—which is lined with delicate membranes and tiny blood vessels that allow the exchange of chemicals between the blood and the air; via the skin—which although mostly waterproof is vulnerable to lipid-soluble substances, and also through cuts and scratches; and via injection—directly into tissue or blood vessels, whether by a hypodermic needle or the fangs of an animal. There are also other routes by which toxins can get into the body, such as via the eyes, but these are much less common.

Many factors determine the likely mode of exposure. Not least among these is the physical state—solid, liquid, or gas—of a poison. For example, a gas is likely to enter the body via the respiratory system, while a solid would probably have to be swallowed. If a poison is in liquid form then its volatility should be considered—in other words, how easily it becomes a vapor. And even a solid can be inhaled if it is in particulate form. In fact, the size of the

A print illustration by François Chauveau of the banquet scene in *Britannicus*, by French playwright Jean Racine (1639–69). The unfortunate Britannicus is succumbing to the poison of his half-brother, the emperor Nero, and his archetypically evil stepmother Agrippina. (See pp. 116–19.)

particles is an important consideration, as small particles can pass deeper into the lungs and are therefore more likely to be absorbed.

Solubility is also crucial. If the toxin is soluble in water, it can easily be swallowed, injected, or come into contact with the skin, but, on the other hand, it will be unlikely to cross the natural barriers of the body such as the lining of the gut. However, poisons become particularly dangerous when lipid-soluble—in other words, when oily or fatty in nature. Lipid-soluble toxins can dissolve in oils and as a result can more easily cross biological barriers, which are generally themselves made out of lipids. These toxins can get through the skin, are more likely to be absorbed through the gut, and are more likely to cross the blood–brain barrier.

The Tragic Case of Professor Wetterhahn

A tragic illustration of the dangers of lipid-soluble toxins is the case of Karen Wetterhahn, a professor at Dartmouth College in New Hampshire. In August 1996 she was working with samples of the compound dimethyl mercury, a form of mercury that is highly toxic and, crucially, lipid-soluble.

Wetterhahn was well aware that the substance she was handling was highly toxic, and as a precaution she was wearing safety glasses and latex gloves and even working under a protective fume hood. As she used a pipette to extract some of the liquid dimethyl mercury from a test tube, a few drops fell onto her hand. Assuming the glove would protect her, she did not immediately take it off—a decision with fatal consequences. While latex is waterproof, lipid-soluble chemicals such as dimethyl mercury can penetrate it, and within seconds a lethal dose had passed through her gloves and into skin.

Once the mercury was in her body, she was doomed, but for reasons that are not understood dimethyl mercury can have a delayed effect. Wetterhahn did not develop symptoms until January 1997, when her feet began to tingle, her gait became unsteady, her speech slurred, and her vision disturbed. Analysis of her blood unveiled over 50 times the toxic threshold of mercury. That February she slipped into a coma, and finally she died in June 1997.

Delivery

Some poisons have malevolent effects at the site of exposure—many snake venoms, for instance, include toxins that break down tissue at the site of the bite. But, as the case of Karen Wetterhahn illustrates, this is rarely the end of the story. If it only affected the exposed site there would be a limit to a toxin's damage. In practice, many only really take effect once they've been delivered to other parts of the body.

The mode of delivery depends on the mode of exposure and in turn affects how much damage the toxin can do and how quickly. For example, ingested toxins follow the same route as digested food, entering the bloodstream through capillaries in the gut wall, which in turn empty into the larger hepatic portal vein—via which they reach the liver before any other parts of the body, with important consequences for their modification (see below). Meanwhile, toxins that are inhaled follow a quite different pathway. Blood from the lungs goes straight to the heart and is then pumped around the rest of the body, and this usually means that inhaled toxins will get to the brain much quicker than ingested ones. Then there are toxins that leach through the skin, and into the blood via the capillaries in the dermis. These usually take longer to get into general circulation, while, on the other hand, injected poisons can enter the bloodstream directly—although obviously a lot depends on the site of injection.

Modification

All bodies incorporate dynamic processes, and even as a toxin is affecting them these processes are themselves modifying the toxin. In this respect, the most important organ is the liver, as part of its function is to detoxify potentially dangerous substances. This process, known as *metabolism*, involves multiple stages, in which a molecule is changed from one intermediate stage—known as a *metabolite*—to another. Unfortunately, some metabolites are toxic themselves, and in some cases a substance becomes toxic only because of metabolism (a process known as *toxication*). One such example is ethanol (alcohol), which is only mildly toxic. However, as the liver breaks it down, it is changed into a metabolite called acetaldehyde, which is much more toxic, and is partly responsible for the painful symptoms of a hangover.

In general, however, liver metabolism is about detoxification. Some toxins are ejected via bile (a fluid produced by the liver) which is fed back into the digestive tract to be carried out with the feces, but the main method of detoxification is by increasing a chemical's solubility in water. The more water-soluble the metabolite, the easier it is for the kidneys—the main organs of excretion—to filter it out of the bloodstream and excrete it via the urine. It's worth noting that kidney function declines with age, so elderly people tend to take longer to excrete toxins, and are therefore vulnerable to higher build-ups over a longer period.

There are, however, also other modes of excretion besides that of the kidneys: as well as the bile produced by the liver, toxins can be expelled via the lungs, or lost in sweat, as well as being shed in skin and hair. And, finally, the immune system also modifies toxins by binding to them and mopping them up before they can damage cells.

Action

Now we find ourselves at the sharp end of toxicology: exactly how toxins are toxic, in other words, how they produce their effects. The mechanisms vary widely and reveal a great deal about the innermost workings of the body. In fact, much of current understanding about molecular, cellular, and physiological processes stems from the study of these toxic mechanisms.

Some poisons achieve their ends outside the cells—among them those that disrupt the communication between nerve and muscle cells. However, most poisons require access, so must make their way through a membrane made of lipids and other molecules to the cell's interior, a task that lipid-soluble toxins perform with relative ease.

Other poisons make use of the cell's own machinery to force entry. One class of molecules, called trans-membrane proteins, are like tiny biological revolving doors—if the right sort of molecule "docks" with it, a

HEROIN

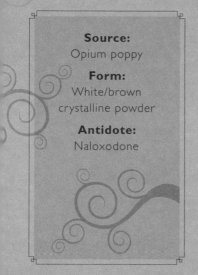

Source:
Opium poppy

Form:
White/brown
crystalline powder

Antidote:
Naloxodone

Overview Heroin is a derivative of morphine (itself a component of opium). First created by Frederick Pierce and his team at St. Mary's Hospital in London in 1874, it is best known as a recreational drug and a painkiller. But it is also an effective poison, and its mechanism is a good illustration of how a toxin works at the molecular level.

Heroin itself is not responsible for most of the effects it produces. Once in the body it is broken down into morphine—the toxic agent. However, heroin is more addictive, powerful, and toxic because it is more lipid-soluble and crosses the blood–brain barrier more easily. The result is that morphine is delivered much more quickly and in larger amounts.

Morphine is what is known as an *agonist*. It binds to and stimulates endorphin receptors, inducing feelings of euphoria, and simultaneously inhibits the release of a pain-signalling molecule. But morphine also binds to receptors in other parts of the brain, including the brainstem, which controls autonomic processes—those not under conscious control, such as breathing, heart rate, blood pressure, and levels of alertness—where it produces its toxic effect.

One of the reasons heroin is so dangerous—it is associated with up to 10,000 deaths per year in the U.S. alone—is that users develop a tolerance. With their endorphin receptors blocked by morphine, neurons generate more receptors, and users need more morphine to produce the same "hit." Addicts become accustomed to larger doses, and, because heroin manufacture is illegal and unregulated, an addict runs the risk of encountering a particularly pure batch and unwittingly giving themselves a lethal dose.

FAMOUS CASES

John Belushi
(1949–82)

Janis Joplin
(1943–70)

River Phoenix
(1970–93)

Symptoms When morphine binds to receptors in the brainstem, it depresses autonomic functions, leading to lethargy, low blood pressure and heart rate, irregularity or cessation of breathing, and eventually coma and death. A characteristic symptom is constriction of the pupils to pinpoints.

Treatment The antidote for an overdose is the antagonist, naloxone, discussed on pp. 32–3.

trans-membrane protein will bring the molecule in through the membrane—and some toxins can fool the trans-membrane proteins into transporting them in this way. Another route through the cell wall are channels, which again are only supposed to admit specific molecules, but can be pried open by certain toxins. Yet another route, one taken by the plant toxin ricin, is for part of the membrane to close around the poison so it is encapsulated in a tiny bag called a *vacuole*, which is itself inside the cell.

Once one has gained access, there are a number of disturbing ways in which a toxin can disrupt or destroy a host cell. Many poisons simply block the expression of a cell's DNA, preventing it from fulfilling the function for which it was made, and this can even undermine the cells of the immune system. Meanwhile, other toxins block the enzymes—complex biological molecules—that catalyze reactions within cells. Furthermore, some take the form of enzymes themselves, and attack molecules within a cell, cutting them to shreds.

Similarly, some poisons, cyanide foremost among them, are able to disrupt the production of ATP (adenosine triphosphate)—a small molecule that provides the energy for the body's biochemistry, and without which a cell will quickly starve. On a related note, processes such as ATP production involve the movement of electrons from one molecule to another; however, this can create molecules with too many electrons, destructive "free radicals" that indiscriminately oxidize and damage other molecules such as DNA. Normally the cell has mechanisms to mop up free radicals and repair damage, but toxins such as mercury can both act as free radicals and disrupt these protective processes, causing cell damage to snowball.

Finally, a further consequence can be the opening of a cell's membrane channels—reminiscent of some toxins' method of forced entry—which can inactivate or hyper-activate nerve and muscle cells, or even cause so much water to flow in that the cell bursts. Such grisly ramifications, albeit on a microscopic scale, require little imagination to extrapolate them to the rest of the body, and it is the stories of these gruesome consequences that dominate the rest of these pages.

The Mad Gassers of Tokyo

On March 20, 1995, 12 people died and over 5,000 people were hospitalized by a nerve-gas attack on the Tokyo subway. A strange and secretive cult called Aum Shinrikyo was accused, but this outrage that shocked the world was only one in a series of strange goings-on.

Aum Shinrikyo, or "Supreme Truth," was founded by the charismatic Shoko Asahara, who claimed to be the first "enlightened one" since Buddha. His mishmash of Buddhism, Hinduism, and apocalyptic prophecies attracted over 40,000 followers and made him enormously rich as cultists were milked for most of their income, forced to work for the cult's businesses, and charged for training courses and Asahara memorabilia including his bathwater, urine, and semen. Many even paid for expensive headsets that supposedly helped them to synchronize their brainwaves with those of the founder.

Members were kept on strict vegetarian diets and abused if they stepped out of line, but Asahara feasted on luxuries. And when the police finally tracked him down by following a trail of melons—a delicacy to which he was addicted— they discovered him cowering in a pod suspended from the ceiling.

Apocalypse Now

A key element of the Aum doctrine was that the end of the world was nigh and that only Aum members would survive. Asahara believed that it was his task to precipitate Armageddon by triggering a new world war, and to accomplish this he initially sought to gain power through an ill-fated run for office in 1989. When this failed, he began to formulate terrorist plots that would destabilize the government, and accordingly Aum began research into weapons of mass destruction, funded by the U.S. $1.5 billion Asahara had accumulated.

Aum cultivated extensive contacts in Russia and used them to acquire weapons technology and expertise. The cult constructed laboratories, and set about researching anthrax, botulin toxins, cholera, and nerve gases. Asahara himself even led a mission to Africa to attempt to bring back samples of the Ebola virus. In the years before the subway atrocity, Aum launched several smaller-scale attacks: releasing the botulin toxin into central Tokyo in 1990 and again in 1993, when they also released anthrax from the top of an office building. But the weaponization and dispersal of such agents is difficult, and these attempts lead only to the deaths of a few pets and birds.

In June 1994, the cult made its first sarin attack. Developed by the Nazis during World War II (see p. 25), sarin could be made using freely available equipment and ingredients. Aum set up several facilities, including one disguised as a Hindu shrine, intending to produce battlefield quantities of nerve gas. Asahara's plan, discovered scrawled on a scrap of paper after his arrest, was for the poison to be released over Japanese cities from two helicopters bought from Russia, while a team of Aum commandos launched a coup. On June 27, 1994, possibly as a training run, a group of cultists in a refrigeration truck drove to Matsumoto—a city to the northwest of Tokyo—and released a cloud of sarin across a residential neighborhood. Seven people were killed and 500 taken to hospital.

What was most incredible about these attacks was the failure of the authorities to detect the cult's activities and take action, despite numerous warnings. Cult members broadcast discussions of attacks on the cult's Russia-based radio station, and there were several cases of the abduction and probable murder of cultists who attempted to leave. Yet Aum was left unmolested. Many conspiracy theorists have smelled a rat, and it has been suggested that Aum had extensive links to the Japanese military, key members of the country's shadowy elite, and the Yakuza, the Japanese mafia. (A profitable sideline for Aum was the use of its laboratories to produce illegal drugs for the Yakuza, and in 1996 the cult's head scientist, Dr. Hideo Murai, was knifed to death by a Yakuza-linked assassin, amid claims of police complicity, supposedly in a bid to stop him revealing details of the operation.) In 1995, however, the authorities finally decided to act, and it is speculated that it was a tip-off from the cult's official connections that prompted Asahara to launch the subway attacks.

Gas Attack

On the morning of March 20, scientists at one of Aum Shinrikyo's chemical weapons facilities filled 11 small plastic bags with liquid sarin and handed them to five cult members, who were to board subway trains on five lines that converged on the city's administrative and political center. The five were driven to the stations, purchasing newspapers on the way and using them to wrap the deadly bags, so that they would look like packed lunches. Each man was also equipped with an umbrella with a sharpened tip.

At approximately 7AM the five men were dropped off at the peak of the morning rush hour. They boarded their trains, took seats, and placed the packages between their feet—standard practice for Japanese commuters. Around an hour later each man pierced his package several times with his umbrella, got off, and went to meet his getaway driver. The five were driven back to Aum headquarters where they were met by Asahari, who congratulated and rewarded them, then told them to vanish.

Meanwhile, the packages were leaking their deadly contents onto the carriage floors, where it evaporated into a cloud of gas. Nearby commuters suffered irritation of the nose and eyes—sarin can be absorbed through the skin and the mucous membranes—but the worst damage was to those who inhaled significant quantities. A single drop of sarin is enough to kill.

Passengers started to cough and vomit, collapsing out of the carriages as the trains pulled into stations. Yet, incredibly, most of the affected trains continued on their way, with passengers getting on even as dying commuters slumped onto the platforms. A commuter on one train, correctly identifying the greasy, stained newspaper package as the source of the noxious fumes, kicked it out of the carriage onto the platform. Subway workers described scenes of carnage, with dozens of bodies littering the ground. In the event, only 12 people died, but many others suffered long-term illness and disability—one woman had to have both eyes removed after her contact lenses were "welded" to her corneas by the gas. In all, nearly 6,000 people were hospitalized, and while most of the victims recovered within a few days, at least one fatality occurred 28 days after the attack. In one example of the insidious nature of nerve agents, several emergency workers and doctors treating victims in an unventilated room also suffered when there was a build-up of fumes from liquid on the victims' clothes.

The End of Aum?

Over the following months the police arrested over 200 cultists and uncovered several chemical weapons sites. Asahara and many of the perpetrators were sentenced to death; most have exhausted the appeals process and await execution. But Asahara's second-in-command, Fumihiro Joyu, escaped with a three-year sentence for perjury, becoming a countercultural hero and teen heartthrob thanks to his media appearances. Upon his release, he took control of the shattered cult and rebranded it as Aleph, later leading a breakaway faction named Hikari no Wa. Despite claims that their aims are peaceful and spiritual, both organizations remain on national and international watchlists.

Meanwhile, conspiracy theorists have had a field day, thanks both to Aum's shadowy connections and evidence that the cult had been pursuing exotic weapons technology such as the particle beam and telegeodynamic (earthquake-generating) weapons dreamed up by eccentric genius Nikola Tesla in the early twentieth century. Shortly before the subway outrage Asahara jetted into Belgrade, apparently hoping to infiltrate the Tesla Museum and steal research papers. After the attacks, attention focused on a ranch that Aum Shinrikyo had purchased in the Australian outback, where in May 1993, just a month after they bought it, an anomalous "seismic detonation" was registered, and witnesses reported seeing a giant fireball. No meteors or earthquakes were recorded by the authorities, and conspiracy theorists believe that it was the test of a Tesla-inspired weapon acquired from the cult's Russian connections.

Another theory is that Aum was just one of several powerful cults to have infiltrated Japanese society at every level, and which share similar apocalyptic visions. Indeed there is evidence that Aum was actually framed for the sarin attack by a rival cult called Soka Gakkai, with even more powerful connections. Perhaps the true masterminds behind the attacks are still at large.

Sarin

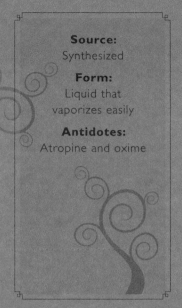

Source:
Synthesized

Form:
Liquid that
vaporizes easily

Antidotes:
Atropine and oxime

Overview Discovered by four German scientists in the early 1940s, sarin derives its name from theirs: Schrader, Ambrose, Rüdiger, and van der Linde. During World War II they developed sarin as a chemical weapon, although by the end of the war it was only being produced on a pilot scale and had not been deployed.

Sarin attacks the enzyme AChE that breaks down the neurotransmitter ACh, which transmits signals across synapses. When ACh binds to a receptor on the target cell it triggers a response (the firing of a nervous impulse or the contraction of a muscle), and unless it is destroyed by AChE it will remain bound to the receptor and continue to trigger the same response.

Symptoms Sarin is absorbed through the skin, mucous membranes, and lungs and quickly reaches the synapses. If encountered as a vapor, the first effects are narrowed pupils, watering eyes, irritation, blurred vision, a runny nose and drooling, sneezing and coughing, a headache, respiratory difficulties, and eventually suffocation. If absorbed through the skin, the first symptoms are sweating and twitching. Symptoms can start within less than a minute.

As the agent spreads there is sweating, nausea and vomiting, incontinence and diarrhea, twitching and jerking, convulsions, confusion, drowsiness, and eventually coma and death. There can be brain damage, but usually death is caused by respiratory failure.

Treatment The body can take weeks or months to generate enough new AChE to restore health. People thought to be at risk (often soldiers) can be given a prophylactic drug, pyridostigmine, in the form of Nerve Agent Protection (NAP) tablets. This also inhibits AChE, but it does so reversibly, so that if a nerve agent attacks the system some of the enzyme will be "sheltered" and then "released." However, interfering with the ACh system has many side effects, and NAP treatments have been blamed for Gulf War Syndrome, a constellation of long-term symptoms.

The antidotes for sarin are atropine (itself a toxin) and oxime. Atropine blocks the ACh receptors, while oxime displaces sarin from being bound to AChE, thus liberating the enzyme to work as normal. Diazepam may also be administered to control convulsions.

Famous Cases

Tokyo subway
gas attack
(1995)

How Much is Too Much?

Every schoolchild wants to know which is the deadliest poison in the world. The answer, predictably, is that it depends. Toxicity is determined above all by the dose that is received, and this depends in turn on a number of other factors. But it also depends on how the dose is presented, the period of time involved, the characteristics of the victim, and several other variables.

But why is the dose so important? The answer is that the response is usually dependent on the dose. This may sound obvious, but it is not necessarily so straightforward, particularly as the dose—response relationship is not always linear (in other words, it is not always the case that twice as much toxin means twice as bad a reaction). This is what the Paracelsus Principle is getting at when it says: "Only the dose determines that a thing is not a poison."

Obviously too much of anything, by definition, is bad for you. Even water can be toxic in large enough doses. Many deaths blamed on ecstasy abuse are actually the result of consuming toxic quantities of water: drink too much and the concentration of vital salts in the blood and tissues becomes too low, while the brain swells and is damaged by the pressure. But, as discussed at the start of the chapter, it is being toxic at a low dose that defines a poison in the normal sense of the word.

There are two types of dose—response relationship. The first is that which is observed within an individual, and is known as the individual or graded response. This is where an individual subject's response to a toxin changes with the dose, and the response is measured in continuous units that change gradually, hence "graded." For instance, researchers might administer increasing amounts of toxin to a mouse and monitor how its blood pressure rises.

The second is the quantal relationship, which is observed across a population and measured using discrete units (usually whether individual subjects live or die). In fact this is often the first test that is done on any newly discovered toxin. A low dose is administered to, for example, 100 mice, followed by a higher dose administered to another 100, and then a higher dose again, and so on. The number that die at each dose is plotted against the dose, which usually results in the "normal distribution" of a bell-shaped graph. This allows researchers to define the dose at which 50 percent of subjects die—known as the LD_{50}, the basic measure of toxicity for any poison.

Hypersusceptibility, Homeostasis, and Hormesis

The dose–response relationship has several important consequences for our understanding of how poisons work. For instance, the normal distribution shown by the quantal relationship means that there will be individuals at either end of the curve who are either resistant or hyper-susceptible. There will also be a threshold dose below which no individuals are killed. Looking at the graded response within an individual can also show some unexpected things. For some substances, such as vitamin A, the individual response curve is U-shaped, showing that when the dose drops below a certain level the response is harmful—in other words, there is a deficiency—but that when it goes above a higher level there is toxicity. Between deficiency and toxicity lies the "region of homeostasis."

A related effect, "hormesis," is where minute quantities of a toxin actually stimulate and boost the health of the subject. For instance, it is suspected that exposing kids to some degree of dirt and germs is actually good for them, because it helps to keep their immune systems in good working order. Similarly, tiny doses of arsenic are known to have a tonic effect on health, and it was even added to livestock feed until relatively recently.

One of the reasons that response depends on dose, and that there is a minimum threshold dose, is that the body has defense systems that allow it to soak up a certain amount of toxic damage. Most cells are equipped with antioxidants, such as vitamins C and E, which neutralize free radicals and prevent oxidative damage (see p. 20). These protective substances provide the body with a sort of toxic buffer, and when they are depleted or exhausted toxins begin to cause toxic damage: the point at which this happens is the dose–response threshold.

Castor Beans and Cassava

Understanding dose is the key to understanding how dangerous a poison may be; but working out the effective dose can be difficult because it involves a great many factors. In short, there is a difference between the dose to which a victim is exposed, and the internal dose that takes effect. At the heart of this discrepancy are many factors such as the route, duration, and timing of exposure, and also differences between the individuals receiving the dose.

The route of exposure can dramatically affect the effective or internal dose. For instance, castor beans—a source of ricin, one of the most toxic substances ever discovered (see pp. 94–5)—are made more toxic by chewing. If the beans are swallowed whole, the testa, or seed coat, which is resistant to digestion, ensures they pass harmlessly through the gut. Similarly, mercury, a highly toxic metal (see pp. 60–5), is extremely dangerous if breathed in as fumes, but is less easily absorbed through the gut. In fact, the margrave of Brandenburg famously drank a large cup of mercury by accident on his wedding night in 1515, and survived unscathed.

Similarly the effect of a dose depends, in part, upon the duration of exposure. At one extreme lies acute exposure, when the subject is exposed to a sudden, high dose of toxin; while at the other lies chronic exposure, where smaller doses accumulate over a long time.

As we have seen previously, individuals themselves also vary widely in their responses to the same dose, and the factors that govern this have an important say in what constitutes an effective dose. Such considerations include health, age, and genetic variations. It is also interesting to note that different species differ widely in their response to toxins, which can make it difficult to extrapolate human reactions from tests on animals; for example, robustoxin, a component of funnel-web spider venom, is extremely dangerous to humans and other primates, but mostly harmless to rabbits.

Furthermore, diet and lifestyle can also radically affect toxicity. One example of this is the case of cassava—a root eaten in many parts of Africa. Unwashed cassava contains high levels of linamarin, which breaks down in the stomach to release cyanide. Healthy individuals usually cope quite well through their normal detoxification processes, but those with a protein-deficient diet are more susceptible and find much lower doses to be toxic. Similarly cadmium, a toxic metal, becomes much more toxic in individuals with a vitamin D deficiency, causing a brittle-bone disease called itai-itai (from the Japanese for "ouch-ouch").

Cellini's Saviors

A graphic illustration of the importance of dose is the extraordinary case of Benvenuto Cellini (1500–71). One of the great sculptors of the Renaissance, a worthy rival to Michelangelo, and the model of the artist as hell-raiser, Cellini was renowned for his whoring and fighting as much as his art, and was said to have enjoyed killing men as much as he enjoyed sculpting. His rapacity led him to contract syphilis by the age of 29, but although he developed the vesicular rash known as "syphilis pox," he declined to undergo the mercury cure offered at that time—as he seems to have understood that it was dangerous in itself.

Untreated, his syphilis progressed to the tertiary stage—when the brain is affected—and it has been speculated that Cellini displayed symptoms of mental imbalance. He concocted grandiose plans, embarked upon dizzyingly ambitious commissions, and displayed signs of megalomania. He was also lured into an ill-advised property scheme, and, according to Cellini's own account, his "partners" decided they could realize their profits earlier if he were dead. They lured him to a dinner at which, he later claimed, he was fed a sauce laced with corrosive sublimate, a form of highly toxic mercury salt that was a favorite of historical poisoners (see Murder in the Tower on pp. 120–2).

Cellini was afflicted with severe gastrointestinal symptoms, including vomiting and diarrhea, and lay grievously ill for days. But although the mercury inflicted severe damage on his gut, it was not sufficient to kill him and he eventually recovered. The dose had, however, been high enough to kill off the parasitic organisms that cause syphilis, and Cellini found himself cured of the terrible disease. He went on to live to a ripe old age, celebrating his would-be assassins as his saviors.

TREATMENTS AND ANTIDOTES

As long as there has been an awareness of poisons, there has also been a pursuit of antidotes. For example, in the tale in which Odysseus's crewmen are poisoned by the sorceress Circe, Homer records the use of "moly," an herbal antidote that guards Odysseus against the witch's brew. Indeed much historical lore about poisons is actually concerned with overcoming them, thereby leading to many strange beliefs and superstitions.

Unicorns' Horns and Toadstones

From ancient authorities such as Pliny and Galen, medieval Europeans derived their belief in the anti-toxic properties of gems and semi-precious stones. Coral, aquamarine, and powdered amethyst were all said to be proof against toxins, while Pliny claimed that diamonds baffled poisons. Medieval traveler and fabulist Sir John Mandeville wrote that "if venom or poison be brought in the presence of the diamond, anon it begins to grow moist and sweat."

Fabulous and semi-magical substances were supposed to have special anti-toxic properties. Foremost among them were bezoars: concretions of minerals retrieved from the stomachs of goats and other animals, a practice derived from the Islamic world, where the *Bad-zahr*—meaning "expelling poison"—cut from the stomach of an antelope-like beast, was said to have the power to neutralize all poisons. Accordingly bezoars were prized possessions of monarchs such as Holy Roman Emperor Charles V and Elizabeth I of England. European monarchs also prized rare "unicorn horns"—usually the horns from narwhals—which were also said to disarm poisons.

More widely available were fossils, ascribed strange lineages and anti-toxic powers. The toadstone was believed to be a semiprecious stone recovered from the forehead or belly of the toad; according to one naturalist the stone could be obtained by seating a toad on a red cloth. In practice the

Circe Pouring Poison into a Vase and Awaiting the Arrival of Ulysses (Odysseus) by English painter Edward Burne-Jones (1833–98).

first toadstones were probably fossilized fish teeth, though later quacks would apply the label to any suitable pebble. The toadstone was believed to warn about the presence of poisons, growing hot in their presence, and stones were set into rings so that they touched the skin of the wearer who could then detect any ominous warming. Similarly, tonguestones—actually fossilized shark's teeth—were believed to neutralize poison.

In modern times, the emergency treatment of poison victims has been radically revised, but techniques had previously remained largely unchanged for over 2,000 years. Dioscorides, a Greek physician serving at Nero's court, was one of the first to record the use of emetics (things that make you vomit) to treat poisoning, and until recently this was standard practice, albeit in the form of gastric lavage, or "stomach-pumping." For any ingested poison, it was assumed that clearing the stomach would limit the dose by preventing further absorption of any poison. Alongside this it was normal to administer activated charcoal (a kind of absorbent soot), and possibly wash the stomach with dilute potassium permanganate, which can neutralize most organic toxins.

The effectiveness of either of these techniques is now questionable, after clinical reviews showed that they did little to improve patient outcome and are risky—emesis, for instance, can cause fluid to enter the airways and lungs. The most up-to-date emergency medics now employ emesis/lavage only in specific circumstances, such as when treating a patient within a very short time of the ingestion of poison.

Instead of aggressive interventions like gastric lavage, the modern emphasis is on stabilizing the patient, alleviating symptoms, and giving the patient's body enough time to detoxify itself. Given sufficient time, and assuming that the dose is not too great or the toxic damage too severe, the liver, kidneys, and other excretory mechanisms will expel most toxins. Emergency treatment therefore focuses on ensuring that breathing is maintained, convulsions are controlled, and plenty of fluids are supplied to replace those lost through vomiting and diarrhea and to flush out the system. Also, a close eye is kept on the blood chemistry so that, for example, excessive alkalinity or acidity can be counteracted. If the kidneys are damaged too badly to filter the blood effectively, dialysis or perfusion can be used as artificial substitutes.

Antidotes

As well as this generic treatment, doctors will try to discover which poison is at work, so that they can administer an antidote—if one exists—that will counteract or interrupt its toxic mechanisms.

Just as there is a huge variety of poisons, there is also a wide array of antidotes to combat them. Some antidotes are generic; for instance, mercury, arsenic, and most heavy metals are treated with an antidote known as a *chelating agent*, which is able to bind to the metal and make it water-soluble and easy to filter out of the blood. However, many antidotes are based on knowledge of the precise mechanism of a toxin, allowing scientists to supply a "magic bullet" to counteract a specific poison. A good example of such a specific treatment is naloxone, the antidote to morphine and heroin. Whereas morphine is an agonist, hyperstimulating the endorphin receptors to which it binds (see p. 19), naloxone is an antagonist that blocks the same receptors and prevents them from firing. Furthermore, naloxone is able to displace morphine from receptors to which it is already bound, reversing the effects of a heroin overdose within minutes.

A type of antidote worthy of special mention is antivenom, or antivenin, which is used to treat cases of animal poisoning, such as snake or spider bites. An antivenom consists of antibodies to the proteins contained in animal venoms, and these antibodies are usually obtained by immunizing an animal such as a horse by exposing it to a tiny quantity of the venom. The creature's immune system will then react by producing antibodies, and these can be harvested from its blood serum for application in human cases. This modern process calls to mind the story of one of history's best-known connoisseurs of antidotes, the legendary Hellenistic king Mithridates the Great (see below).

Perhaps the most legendary formulation of antidotes—one used from Roman times to the Renaissance and beyond—was Mithridatum or Mithridate. Reputed to defeat all poisons this mystical concoction took its name from Mithridates the Great (132–63 BC), a king who had a justifiable fear of poisoning and determined to make himself invulnerable by the regular consumption of antidotes. In fact, Pliny records that Mithridates even dosed himself with poisons to build up his resistance.

However, Mithridates' wariness was to rebound upon him. With his kingdom overrun by the Roman legions of Pompey, this great thorn in the empire's flank attempted to avoid capture by swallowing poison. But, thanks to his precautions, it was ineffective and he was forced to rely on cold steel. In spite of his unfortunate fate, Mithridates' recipe for antidotes was supposedly taken back to Rome, while his name lives on in the term *mithradatic* meaning "of or concerning antidotes."

CHAPTER TWO

POISON

IN

NATURE

> "There is poison in the fang of the serpent, in the mouth of the fly, and in the sting of the scorpion; but the wicked man is saturated with it."

Chanakya (c. 350–283 BC), *Arthastra*

THE NATURAL WORLD IS FULL OF POISONS. NATURALLY OCCURRING TOXINS RANGE FROM INORGANIC ELEMENTS AND MINERALS AND TOXINS SYNTHESIZED BY MICROORGANISMS TO FACILITATE THEIR LIFE CYCLES, TO POISONS PRODUCED BY PLANTS TO PROTECT THEMSELVES AND VENOMS USED BY ANIMALS FOR BOTH DEFENSE AND ATTACK. NATURE HAS EXPERIMENTED WITH A PROFUSION OF POISONS, AND FOR THE GREATER PART OF HISTORY THESE WERE THE ONLY ONES AVAILABLE TO HUMANITY. ACCORDINGLY, A RICH STORE OF EXPERIENCE, LORE, AND MISADVENTURE HAS GROWN UP AROUND ANIMAL, MINERAL, AND VEGETABLE TOXINS, FROM THEIR ANCIENT USES AND ABUSES TO THE LATEST MOLECULAR AND GENETIC RESEARCH.

As the great fourth-century BC sage and statesman Chanakya understood, while nature may invent poisons it is humans who turn them to the cruellest ends. According to legend, Chanakya (c. 350–283 BC) was well placed to understand the perils and pitfalls of poison. In a tale that recalls the legend of Mithridates (see p. 33), Chanakya attempted to protect his master and protégé, the first Maurya emperor Chandragupta, by regularly feeding him sub-lethal doses of toxins, so that he would become immune to assassination by poison. But, almost inevitably, Chanakya's strategy had unexpected consequences, and when the emperor unwittingly shared his poison-laced food with his wife, she was killed. The identity of the fatal substance has not come down to us, but as the following chapter will illustrate, Chanakya could have chosen from a galaxy of natural choices.

POISONOUS CREATURES

The range of poisonous animals is astonishing; venomous or poisonous creatures are known from every major class of animal, from unicellular protozoans to mammals such as the short-tailed shrew and the duck-billed platypus. According to *Casarett & Doull's Toxicology*—the "bible" of toxicology: "Although there are no exact figures on the numbers of such animals, there are approximately 1,200 species of venomous or poisonous marine animals, countless venomous arthropods [the class that includes insects, spiders, and scorpions], and about 400 species of snake considered dangerous to humans." Indeed the latest research into the evolution of toxins in snakes (see right) suggests that, in reptiles at least, these figures could be even higher.

Venomous versus Poisonous

Before looking at individual creatures, it's worth distinguishing between those that are venomous and those that are merely poisonous. Essentially, being venomous is an active property, while being poisonous is passive.

Venomous animals are those that actively deploy poison in defense or attack, delivering it by biting or stinging. They concoct their poisons in specialized glands and store it in special structures until it can be deployed via fangs, stingers, or spines. (It's interesting to note that offensive venoms tend to be associated the "oral pole," or mouth end, of a creature, while defensive ones are associated with the "aboral pole," the back end.)

Poisonous animals, by contrast, are those with tissues that are partly or wholly toxic, but which have no means of actively deploying their toxins. Some poisonous animals may even be incidentally or non-functionally poisonous. For instance, toxins can build up or "bio-accumulate" in the body of an animal because they are present in its diet, and one such example is the bio-accumulation of mercury by some swordfish.

Snakes and the Evolution of Venom

Given their classical and mythological links to poison, it is hardly surprising that snakes have been the focus of research into the evolution of venoms. And recent findings have uncovered fascinating secrets about how and when snake venoms evolved. Leading evolutionary toxicologist Dr. Bryan Grieg Fry, of the University of Melbourne, says that the most ancient snakes were probably big, heavy "swamp monsters," and like today's anaconda used their bodies and perhaps big teeth to catch their prey. But as their prey evolved to become faster and more agile, so snakes also had to adapt, swapping their sluggish muscularity for a more refined tool: venom. Adaptations such as fangs, usually with a groove to conduct venom deep into the bite wound, only arose after the evolution of potent toxins, as a way to increase their lethality.

However, Fry has also been involved in research that suggests venom evolved even earlier than the first snake. What's more, genetic comparison of the toxins produced by lizards and snakes shows they are related, suggesting that there was "a single, early origin of the venom system."

One consequence of this is that snakes that were previously considered non-venomous are now thought to have evolved from venomous ancestors, and may even still possess venoms or at least the ability to make them. Sure enough, when Fry looked at the ratsnake, a common pet, he discovered that its saliva contained a highly potent neurotoxin also found in cobra venom. Fortunately ratsnakes do not produce venom in cobra-like quantities or have the ability to deliver it with a vicious set of fangs, but those who keep them as pets may care to consider that their companions are still producing deadly poisons.

Snake venoms typically consist of a mixture of toxic proteins with some inorganic elements, and sometimes also organic molecules such as lipids and carbohydrates. However, it is usually proteins that are the active ingredients, launching multiple attacks on the physiology of the victim: breaking down the flesh at the site of a bite; causing muscle weakness, paralysis, and respiratory failure; damaging blood cells; and causing the cardiovascular system to fail. At the same time other toxic proteins disrupt the clotting system of the blood, so that victims may even bleed to death via the bite.

What is the Most Poisonous Snake?

This is a very different question to "What is the most dangerous snake?" or "Which snake kills the most people?" Answers to such questions are determined only in part by the poison, but more by external factors such as the range of the species, its habitat, level of human contact, and the availability of antivenins and the general provision of healthcare. Factors like these, and not the comparative toxicity of the venom of snake species in each region, mean that in North America there are only around 12–15 deaths from snake bite each year, while in India and Pakistan the number is around 50,000–70,000.

Given all these caveats, is it possible to say which snake has the most potent venom? Well, measures have been derived for many species by giving mice subcutaneous injections, and according to this mode, the snake with the most toxic venom is the inland taipan, *Oxyuranus microlepidotus*, also known as the fierce or small-scaled snake. A single bite from the inland taipan can contain enough venom to kill 100 human adults or up to 250,000 mice, and it is over 50 times more toxic than the venom of a king cobra. Fortunately this snake is restricted to arid central Australia, and, despite its alternative name and impressive size—typically around 6½ ft (2 m)—it is docile unless provoked. It

As they are produced by oral glands, it had been thought that venom toxins probably evolved from saliva. In fact, most prove to have derived from proteins normally found elsewhere in the body. Evolution took proteins from such places as the heart, liver, muscle, brain, and eye and modified them so that they could be used against the related organs in the bodies of prey. Neurotoxins, for instance, may be a form of modified neurotransmitter. This may help to account for the remarkable variety, specificity, and potency of snake toxins.

normally feeds on small rodents, and although its bite could easily kill a person, there are no recorded instances of anyone dying, largely thanks to the availability of antivenin. The table below, based on data compiled by Dr. Bryan Grieg Fry, shows the subcutaneous LD_{50}s (see pp. 26–7) for some of the best-known and most toxic snakes:

Common name	Scientific name	LD_{50} (mg/kg)
Inland taipan	Oxyuranus microlepidotus	0.025
Eastern brown snake	Pseudonaja textilis	0.0365
Dubois's sea snake	Aipysurus duboisii	0.044
Coastal taipan	Oxyuranus scutellatus	0.106
Tiger rattlesnake	Crotalus tigris	0.21
Olive sea snake	Aipysurus laevi	0.264
Black mamba	Dendroaspis polylepsis	0.32
Spectacled cobra	Naja naja	0.45
Egyptian cobra	Naja haje	1.15
King cobra	Ophiophagus hannah	1.7
Adder	Vipera berus	6.45
Eastern diamondback rattlesnake	Crotalus adamanteus	14.6
Cottonmouth/ Water moccasin	Agkistrodon piscivorus	25.8

To complicate matters further, different species produce and deliver widely varying quantities of venom. For example, although the eastern brown snake is two and a half times more toxic than the coastal taipan, the latter delivers up to 30 times more venom with each strike, making its bite up to 12 times more deadly. Even individual snakes vary in the amount of venom they deliver from strike to strike. In fact, a snake rarely injects all its venom in one go, and the proportion expended in a single bite depends on age, aggressiveness, and an assessment of the threat. For example, an older snake that is not alarmed may choose not to inject any venom at all, and studies of the Malaysian cobra have found that only 13 percent of bites resulted in envenomation.

Treating Snakebites

Hollywood has immortalized the traditional response to a snakebite: a shallow cut is made from fang point to fang point, and the venom sucked out. However, even if done properly, this is likely to extract little venom, and the more the sucker extracts the more likely he or she is to be poisoned. The most likely outcome is simply that the wound is exacerbated.

A more popular, albeit no more effective, remedy in the nineteenth century was alcohol, for it was believed that whiskey or brandy were proof against venoms. However, it proved to have unpredictable consequences, as one frontier physician reported he had treated a rattlesnake-bite victim with a gallon and a half of whiskey over a 36-hour period, only to find that when the victim recovered he promptly went out in search of another rattlesnake to get bitten by. Drunkenness aside, alcohol is counterproductive, as it increases the blood flow and accelerates the spread of venom.

So what should you do if someone is bitten? Well, the most important thing is to seek medical attention as soon as possible. The victim should also try to move as little as possible, in order to slow the spread of venom, and keep the bite lower than the heart. Tourniquets are not generally advised, but if the snake is very venomous and medical attention is likely to arrive quickly, they can be worth trying. You should also note the identity—or at least appearance—of the snake that gave the bite, so an antivenin can be administered. In fact, most fatalities result from the failure to give the correct antivenin, or from giving too small a dose of it. That said, antivenins themselves pose risks through extreme immune reactions such as anaphylaxis, the flu-like "serum sickness," and also kidney problems. Accordingly, some doctors prefer to wait to see if an antivenin is absolutely necessary before administering it.

Spiders and Scorpions

Foremost among the other venomous creatures are spiders and scorpions. And it may compound many people's arachnophobia to discover that most of the world's spider species are in fact venomous to some extent—of the 20,000 species in the U.S. only two are not venomous. In fact, some 200 species worldwide have been implicated in serious incidents with humans, but most spiders do not have fangs big enough to pierce human skin.

Spider venom has evolved both to immobilize its prey, normally an insect or small creature, and to break down and liquefy the tissues so the spider can suck the juices up. To accomplish their dual ends, spiders use a range of toxins, often working in synergy. And even primitive species make up to 50 different toxins, some of which are highly specific; for instance, the species *Nephila clavata* targets receptors on specific neurons in the hippocampus in the brain, and a bite from this species can lead to memory problems.

Although spider bites may feel as harmless as those of ants, unpleasant symptoms can soon follow. For example, a bite from a Sydney funnel-web spider can cause circulatory failure, breathlessness, salivation, sweating, and pain; while a bite from a black widow or its Australian equivalent, the red-back, initially causes vomiting, abdominal pain, and sweating, leading to cramps, twitching, and paralysis. A funnel-web bite can kill within 15 minutes, while the victim of a red-back can suffer symptoms lasting over two months. Fortunately only a small proportion of bites cause severe poisoning—of the 2,000 people bitten annually by the red-back, only 20 percent are seriously affected. The main treatment is antivenin, together with antibiotics, corticosteroids, ice packs, and rest.

Tarantulas play upon the popular consciousness, but are really only mildly toxic to humans. In southeastern Europe it was traditionally believed that their bite caused a hysterical condition, tarantism, related to a folk dance called the tarantella, which was variously believed to be either a symptom or a cure.

Like the spider, the scorpion looms large in the popular imagination of deadly creatures; but although all are poisonous only some 75 species are medically important. Generally, a scorpion cannot deliver enough venom to kill a healthy person, although the elderly and children are at greater risk, and there is also some risk from anaphylactic shock. The only useful treatment for a scorpion sting is antivenin.

Other venomous, albeit less feared, arthropods include the Hymenoptera (bees, wasps, and ants), and ticks and mites. The latter can cause tick paralysis because of their venom, and should be removed if discovered biting. Great care must be taken in this however, as simply pulling can cause the jaws to break off in the wound—the best way to get rid of a tick is with gasoline or a pair of flat-tip forceps wielded with a rotating motion. Surprisingly, in the developed world the Hymenoptera are responsible for more deaths than any other venomous creature, but this is mainly the result of anaphylactic reactions, rather than the toxicity of their venom itself. However, it is still possible that bee venom can be fatal to people who are not specifically sensitive to it, but it will take more than a hundred stings to kill an adult.

Poisonous Frogs and Toads

Moving away from venoms, many amphibians use toxicity to discourage predators, and possibly also to protect themselves from bacteria—frogs that are prevented from making skin poisons are more likely to become infected and die. Intriguing research shows that poisonous frogs do not make these toxins themselves, but derive them from their diet. And research on strawberry dart-poison frogs in Costa Rica shows that their toxins come primarily from oribatid mites that live in the soil. The frogs are able to absorb the poisons through their guts and sequester them in skin poison glands, while frogs reared in captivity, without access to mites, do not have this toxic defense.

Amazingly, nearly 300 different toxins have been isolated from frogs, newts, and toads, including batrachotoxin, one of the most potent poisons known, and bufotenin, a hallucinogen, responsible for the dangerous phenomenon of teenagers licking the backs of cane toads in order to get high.

CANTHARIDES

Source:

The Spanish fly beetle, *Cantharis* or *Lytta vesicatoria*; or in the East, the Chinese or Indian blistering beetle, *Mylabris sidea*

Form:
White powder

Antidote:
None

Overview Also known as Spanish fly, the most notorious aphrodisiac in history, cantharides is derived from an iridescent green beetle commonly found on olive trees and honeysuckles. The beetle is rich in cantharidin, which is an irritant and also causes the blood vessels to widen. The latter effect can help to produce erections, while the former causes irritation in the urethra, which the sufferer then seeks to relieve through intercourse. Until recently, cantharides has been an important tool in animal husbandry, but as a human aphrodisiac it is painful, dangerous, and unreliable.

However, this has not stopped people trying to use it throughout the ages. It was an ingredient in a love philtre cooked up by seventeenth-century French witch and poisoner la Voisin (see pp. 144–5), while the Marquis de Sade claimed to have fed Spanish-fly laced pastilles to prostitutes. More recently, in London in 1954, office worker Arthur Ford dosed two colleagues with cantharides-laced candy, apparently believing it would work like a love philter. The two women died, but Ford survived to stand trial.

Cantharides was used medically as a vesicant—a blistering agent. And one such example was in the form of Liquor Epispasticus, which was to be painted on to the skin, to supposedly ease the pain of congested joints. It was also used variously in hair lotions, as a scalp stimulant, and to trigger abortions.

Symptoms The toxin irritates anything it comes into contact with, causing burning pain in the mouth and throat, vomiting, colic, bloody diarrhea and urine, irritation of the urethra, blistering of skin and mucous membranes, bleeding, collapsing blood pressure, coma, and death. One of the traditional tests for cantharides poisoning was the vesication test, where organs of a suspected victim were used to make an ointment, which was then rubbed on the shaven skin of a live rabbit, which would then blister.

Treatment There is no antidote, and little available treatment beyond attempting to ameliorate the victim's symptoms.

FAMOUS CASES

Livia
(c. 58–29 BC)

Marquise de Brinvilliers
(1630–76)

Marquis de Sade
(1740–1814)

The Arthur Ford Case
(1954)

Poisonous Marine Animals

There are around 1,200 venomous or poisonous marine animals, and they include some of the nastiest and most toxic of venomous critters. At the bottom of the food chain are single-celled creatures that produce toxins, and these are indirectly responsible for the most dangerous—in terms of death toll—of poisonous marine animals. When fish and shellfish eat these toxic animalcules they absorb their poisons; the more they eat, the more toxins they accumulate, in a process known as bio-accumulation or biomagnification.

At certain times of year shellfish accumulate high levels of these toxins and become dangerous to eat; mussels in particular become contaminated with paralytic shellfish poison (PSP), a blend of toxins. Mild illness can be brought on by 1 mg of PSP, which could be supplied by just one mussel or clam; 4 mg would probably be fatal.

The most infamous of poisonous sea animals are the jellyfish. These strange creatures trail tentacles equipped with nematocysts—tiny cells packed with poison and apparatus for deploying it. These nematocysts evolved to immobilize and kill prey, but they also pose a particularly horrible hazard to human bathers. Sticky tentacles adhere to the skin and attempts to brush or pull them off simply cause more nematocysts to fire—the correct way to get rid of them is to pour alcohol on them. Ugly, livid welts appear,

When ocean conditions are right or there is fertilizer run-off from the land, huge blooms of toxic single-celled creatures—such as the *Gymnodinium* genus of dinoflagellate shown here at a magnification of 12,000—result in "red tides." Local seafood accumulates high levels of toxins, and this leads to ciguatera poisoning, which can be a major public health risk, especially in the Caribbean and South Pacific.

and toxins including neurotoxins and blood-cell bursting proteins can be fatal within minutes, in the case of the most dangerous jellyfish, the sea wasp.

Less well known are the cone snails that live in brightly colored cone-shaped cells up to 8 in (20 cm) long. They have harpoon-like teeth that can pierce thin cloth, and which inject highly potent neurotoxins, which can kill by respiratory paralysis within a few hours, although they usually only bite people who are handling them. Cone snails are especially interesting because their toxins have been researched extensively for biomedical applications, and may result in powerful new painkillers (see p. 209).

Another venomous mollusk is the tiny but potent blue-ringed octopus—the eponymous blue bands glow to signal the imminent release of its poison, although this only happens if the creature is handled or disturbed. The primary toxin of the blue-ringed octopus is maculotoxin, which is identical to tetrodotoxin, the potent poison found mainly in the liver and gonads of the pufferfish or fugu.

Eaten as a delicacy in Japan, fugu famously has to be prepared by highly trained chefs (*fugu chirishii menkyo*) to ensure that the flesh is not contaminated with tetrodotoxin. This toxin disrupts nerve firing and affects muscle cells, causing paralysis, low blood pressure, and respiratory failure—a fate which awaits around 125 people a year. Reports of tetrodotoxin's toxicity and lethality vary: according to some sources the LD_{50} is as low as 0.008 mg per kg, with a mortality rate of over 40 percent for those who ingest it; while others claim it substantially less toxic at 0.1 mg per kg.

According to research by ethnobotanist Wade Davis, tetrodotoxin is one of the active ingredients in *coup de poudre*, a powder used by voodoo magicians as the first step toward creating a zombie. Supposedly it is used to depress respiration and heart rate in the victim in order to give the appearance of death. Once these effects have taken hold the victim is buried alive, before later being exhumed and fed psychoactive drugs that will complete the process. However, this claim has been widely dismissed as either folklore or fiction, not least because the paralysis and floppy limbs symptomatic of tetrodotoxin poisoning do not match the characteristically jerky movements of zombification.

Bacteria and Molds

The human gut is full of billions of bacteria, which are essential for its proper functioning; but some strains can turn nasty and cause food poisoning and other diseases, such as shigellosis and cholera.

Typical symptoms of food poisoning are gastrointestinal discomfort, malaise, fever, and diarrhea progressing to watery dysentery, which in extreme cases is known as "rice water" dysentery, because the slightly cloudy fluid resembles water used to wash rice. The people most at risk are those with disturbed or vulnerable gut flora, including infants and the elderly, and people with suppressed immune function. Antibiotics can kill most bacteria, but the most important treatment is replacement of lost fluids and electrolytes.

The Case of Cholera

Cholera is an infamous epidemic disease caused by the spread of the bacterium *Vibrio cholerae* through contaminated drinking water. Once the bacterium gets into the gut it swims through the intestinal mucus and attaches itself to the cells of the gut lining, where it starts to produce an enterotoxin. This alters the membranes of the gut cells, causing them to pump chlorine ions into the gut, which in turn draws up massive amounts of water to be expelled as dysentery. The dehydration that results can kill in as little as three hours.

Long restricted to India, cholera began to spread around the world in a series of massive pandemics in the nineteenth century, claiming hundreds of thousands of lives as it went. But these tragedies did prompt an important contribution to human civilization. In 1854, the English physician John Snow traced a cholera outbreak to a water pump, and realized that the disease was caused by contaminated water rather than the previously assumed "miasma." It was this realization that prompted the development of sewers and other public health systems in the developed world.

BOTULINUM

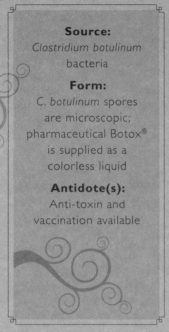

Source:

Clostridium botulinum
bacteria

Form:

C. botulinum spores
are microscopic;
pharmaceutical Botox®
is supplied as a
colorless liquid

Antidote(s):

Anti-toxin and
vaccination available

Overview

Botulinum toxin is the most potent known toxin—just a few hundred grams would be enough to kill every human on the planet.

The toxin is produced by a bacterium, *Clostridium botulinum*, which is anaerobic, meaning it can only grow in oxygen-free conditions. Although found ubiquitously in the soil, *C. botulinum* is only a threat in specific circumstances: via contaminated food which has been canned or bottled; in poorly dressed wounds; nd occasionally in the digestive system of infants.

Botulinum toxin is made up of seven separate toxins, of which type A is the most important in humans. It is a large protein, with one part that binds to nerve cells and smuggles the toxin inside, while the other attacks the tiny sacs that contain neurotransmitters, completely blocking nerve function.

Symptoms

The usual symptoms on ingestion of contaminated food are difficulty in speaking and swallowing and blurred vision. Weakness and paralysis spread from the upper limbs and trunk to the lower limbs. There may be vomiting, gastrointestinal upset, constipation, a dry mouth, and high blood pressure, but the brain, senses, and consciousness are mostly unaffected. Death is usually due to respiratory paralysis. Wound botulism shows similar progression but without gastrointestinal symptoms, while in infant botulism there is general lethargy and weakness, with expressionless features.

Treatment

The first recorded outbreak was in Wildbad, Germany, in 1793, where it was traced back to contaminated blood sausage—the name derives from *botulus*, Latin for "sausage." Crucially the food was uncooked, as botulinum is easily deactivated by heat, making cooking the best preventative measure. However, anti-toxin and vaccines are available.

The paralyzing effects of botulinum can last for months, so that it can be used in minute quantities to treat problematic nerve and muscle function—for instance, in cases of squint, cerebral palsy, writer's cramp, and many neurological disorders. As Botox®, botulinum A can also be used to paralyze small facial muscles and thus diminish wrinkles, although very precise application is required.

FAMOUS CASES

Wildbad, Germany,
"Sausage poisoning"
outbreak
(1793)

POISONOUS PLANTS

Thousands of species of plants make poisons to discourage animals from eating them. As a result plants produce a vast range of pharmacologically active chemicals, and until the advent of industrial chemistry humans depended on plants for access to most of their therapeutic drugs and harmful toxins (often one and the same, differentiated only by dose). Indeed evidence from the animal world suggests that humans have been taking advantage of the pharmaceutical, and therefore toxic, properties of plants since they first evolved. Gorillas, chimps, and many other animals have been observed in the wild apparently medicating themselves with pharmacologically active plants, such as purgatives that help flush out intestinal parasites. Presumably the earliest hominids possessed similar abilities, so that as long as there have been humans there have been poisoners.

Accidental poisoning through consumption probably has a similarly long history, and until the ninteenth century this was far and away the most common form of poisoning. At the beginning of the nineteenth century over 90 percent of cases of poisoning were linked to plants. Today, thanks to the abundance of synthesized poisons, this has dropped to just 7 per cent.

Plant Toxicity

A problem that faced doctors in the era before the artificial synthesis of pharmaceuticals—and which still troubles herbalists, practitioners of Chinese medicine, and others today—is that plant preparations vary widely in toxicity from one batch to the next. This variability greatly increases the danger of accidental poisoning.

Plant toxicity varies because of several factors. Toxins may be concentrated to different extents in different parts of the plant. In the castor-oil plant, for instance, ricin is almost entirely concentrated in the castor bean; while in the

Strychnos nux-vomica plant, strychnine is present in the stem, bark, and seeds. Toxicity also varies over the lifetime of a plant—young pokeweed shoots, for instance, can be eaten in a salad, but berries and leaves from a mature plant can cause gastrointestinal problems. The climate, soil conditions, and season also affect the growth of particular plants and therefore the amount of toxins they produce. For example, the fruit of the mandrake can be safely eaten when it is ripe enough, but is extremely dangerous at other times. Meanwhile, the varied response of individuals to a toxin (see pp. 26–8) is echoed by the genetic differences between individual plants of the same species; so that one plant may be nearly harmless but its neighbor highly toxic.

Jimsonweed and "Natural Fools"

Datura stramonium is a common weed, related to the more widely known deadly nightshade. Like many potent plants it has accumulated a plethora of wild and wonderful names, including angel's trumpet, mad apple, stink weed, Devil's trumpet, thorn apple, hell's bells, and jimsonweed. In fact, the latter derives from the most famous incident of datura poisoning, when British soldiers sent to Jamestown in Virginia in 1676, to suppress an uprising known as Bacon's Rebellion, were poisoned en masse with the plant—sources disagree whether this was by wily colonists or by accident.

As with many poisonous plants, human use of *Datura stramonium* dates back to prehistoric times. The genus name, *Datura*, derives from a Sanskrit word, alluding to the ancient use of the plant by Hindu Sadhus. The species name *stramonium* derives from the Greek roots *strychnos* "nightshade" and *manikos* "mad."

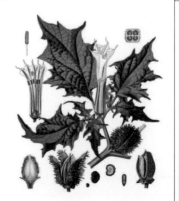

BELLADONNA

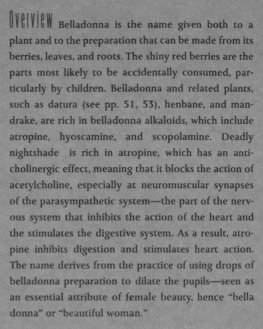

Source:
Atropa belladonna, also known as deadly nightshade, Devil's cherries, Devil's herb, and dwale

Form:
The whole plant is poisonous, but especially the berries

Antidote(s):
No specific antidote, but physostigmine may be used to counteract some effects

Overview

Belladonna is the name given both to a plant and to the preparation that can be made from its berries, leaves, and roots. The shiny red berries are the parts most likely to be accidentally consumed, particularly by children. Belladonna and related plants, such as datura (see pp. 51, 53), henbane, and mandrake, are rich in belladonna alkaloids, which include atropine, hyoscamine, and scopolamine. Deadly nightshade is rich in atropine, which has an anticholinergic effect, meaning that it blocks the action of acetylcholine, especially at neuromuscular synapses of the parasympathetic system—the part of the nervous system that inhibits the action of the heart and the stimulates the digestive system. As a result, atropine inhibits digestion and stimulates heart action. The name derives from the practice of using drops of belladonna preparation to dilate the pupils—seen as an essential attribute of female beauty, hence "bella donna" or "beautiful woman."

Symptoms

Characteristic symptoms of belladonna poisoning are loss of voice and loss of movement of the hands and fingers. In small doses atropine can be used to halt stomach or gut spasms, dilate pupils, and speed up the heart. In toxic doses it causes extreme dryness of the mouth and throat, urinary retention, and racing pulse. The pupils may also become very dilated, interfering with vision. Victims become excitable, paranoid, and delirious, losing their sense of reality. Eventually there may be fever, convulsions, respiratory paralysis, coma, and death; or, on recovery, amnesia and depression. There may be a rash, especially on the upper body.

Treatment

Emetics and gastric lavage are indicated if berries have very recently been swallowed. Other treatments may include physostigmine, stimulants, valium, and even coffee. Atropine and other belladonna alkaloids are medically important; they are used as sedatives and antispasmodics. Belladonna extracts were once used in cough medicine.

FAMOUS CASES

Roman emperor
Augustus
(27 BC – AD 19)

Dr. Crippen
(1862–1910)

Like belladonna, datura is rich in tropane alkaloids, which, apart from their physical effects such as a dry mouth and dilated pupils, also have potent hallucinogenic effects. Alkaloids such as scopolamine are capable of inducing "true hallucinations"—those that cannot be distinguished from reality—as Robert Beverly's famous account of the Jamestown poisoning, in his 1705 *The History and Present State of Virginia*, makes clear:

> "Some of the soldiers sent thither to quell the rebellion of Bacon . . . ate plentifully of it, the effect of which was a very pleasant comedy, for they turned natural fools upon it for several days: one would blow up a feather in the air; another would dart straws at it with much fury; and another, stark naked, was sitting up in a corner like a monkey, grinning and making [faces] at them; a fourth would fondly kiss and paw his companions, and sneer in their faces with a countenance more antic than any in a Dutch droll.

> "In this frantic condition they were confined, lest they should, in their folly, destroy themselves—though it was observed that all their actions were full of innocence and good nature. Indeed, they were not very cleanly; for they would have wallowed in their own excrements, if they had not been prevented. A thousand such simple tricks they played, and after 11 days returned themselves again, not remembering anything that had passed."

Vanishing Cigarettes

Datura's reputation as a natural hallucinogen persists, with the result that each year in America sees hundreds of teenagers admitted to emergency rooms having smoked or eaten the plant. Common hallucinations of mild doses of datura include interaction with non-existent objects, especially cigarettes, and many users find that the cigarette they thought they were smoking has vanished. Scopolamine in particular is absorbed into the central nervous system erratically, over a long period of time, so that users can easily be fooled into taking more than the safe dose. Treatment for overdosers is similar to that for atropine or belladonna poisoning.

Poisonous Fungi

Fungi range in size from single-celled molds to mushrooms and toadstools—"toadstool" being a traditional name for a toxic mushroom—and toxic fungi are known from both ends of this spectrum. Fungi are a popular food source in many parts of the world, but one that poses considerable dangers, as poisonous and non-poisonous species can be easily confused. The vast majority of deaths by poison mushroom are due to the death cap, *Amanita phalloides*; in the United States, for instance, it is responsible for over 90 percent of fatal mushroom poisonings. Also dangerous are destroying angels (*Amanita virosa/ocreata*) and the fly agaric (*Amanita muscaria*), the unusual name of which derives from its being fatal to flies when steeped in milk or water. Basically, all *Amanita* mushrooms are

to be avoided, although there are also a number of other toxic genera such as *Cortinarius* and *Lepiota*.

The main toxins produced by fungi are mycotoxins, produced by molds, which include aflatoxins (see p. 56) and ergot (see p. 58); and phallotoxins and amatoxins (see p. 57). Fly agaric also contains potent hallucinogens, and has therefore been used since prehistoric times—one theory has the notorious Viking berserkers dosing up on the fungus before plunging into battle—taking its place alongside other sacred toxic intoxicants such as mandrake, henbane, the opium poppy, cannabis, and belladonna. It is suggested that this association with the mystical and magical could also be the root of the association between toadstools and fairies.

How to Tell a Mushroom from a Toadstool

There are many folkloric and dangerously inaccurate beliefs about how to tell mushrooms from toadstools. It is not true, for instance, that they are easily told apart, or that toadstools are distinguished by bright colors and patterns, foul smell or taste, or the absence of insects and other animals. Boiling a toadstool in water and vinegar will not detoxify it, and even thorough cooking does not inactivate all the toxins. Cutting a mushroom open and rubbing it on a silver coin may indeed result in the silver being darkened by formation of hydrogen cyanide or sulfide, but this happens with both edible and inedible mushrooms, though not necessarily with all toxic species. Neither will employing a dog or pig to hunt for fungi ensure they are edible; even if the animal eats some and seems fine, this is no guarantee of a person's safety, as toxic effects can take hours to appear.

This illustration from the classic german encyclopedia *Meyers Konversations-Lexikon* (fourth edition; 1897) shows a selection of poisonous mushrooms, ranging from the stereotypical toadstool of folklore—the classic example of which is the fly agaric (*Amanita muscaria*), shown bottom center—to varieties that resemble edible fungi.

Identification can be achieved by carefully checking several variables such as cap color, gill color, stalk shape, season—for example, *Amanita* species flourish in the autumn—and habitat. Experts can tell from the color of the spores, which can be checked by placing a cut mushroom on a piece of half-light, half-dark paper. However, the general rule is that if you are in any doubt whatsoever you should avoid consuming the fungus in question.

Mold and Aflatoxin

Less obvious, but more insidious, are poisonous molds, of which one example is *Aspergillus flavus*. This grows on peanuts and other grains in hot and humid climates, and produces aflatoxins, which threaten the health of any animals eating contaminated nuts or grain. The threat that aflatoxin posed was first discovered in 1960 when a mysterious ailment dubbed Turkey X Syndrome struck down more than 100,000 birds in the U.K. All had been fed with a feed made from peanuts, or ground nuts, which were later shown to be contaminated with aspergillus mold. The dead birds showed damage to their livers, and particularly cancers.

Since then more research has shown that aflatoxins are also dangerous to humans, and indeed that there is a higher rate of liver cancer in areas where grains and nuts are susceptible to aspergillus mold—most notably among Bantu tribespeople in Africa, who prefer their corn to be moldy. In humans the most dangerous form is aflatoxin B1, which is metabolized by the liver into a highly oxidative metabolite. This damages the DNA of liver cells, producing hepatitis in the case of acute poisoning, and a carcinogenic effect in cases of chronic exposure. In fact, aflatoxins are among the most potent carcinogens known. There is also evidence that genetic factors and exposure to the virus that causes hepatitis B greatly increase susceptibility.

Treatment of affected crops with fungicide can control the aspergillus mold, but the growing demand for organic foods may present problems. Organic peanut butter, for instance, is more likely to be contaminated with aflatoxins than normally processed brands.

THE DEATH CAP

Source:

Amanita phalloides

Form:

Cap color depends on location—snow-white, pale green, or tan particularly poisonous; white gills; bulbous stalk base; white spore print

Antidote:

Milk-thistle extract with silymarin

Overview

As its sinister name might suggest, this one species is responsible for most of the world's deaths by fungal poisoning. Its deadly properties have been known since ancient times, and Pliny mentions cases of death-cap poisoning.

Apart from its extreme toxicity, one of the things that makes this fungus dangerous is its resemblance to some edible mushrooms. Southeast Asian immigrants to the U.S. are at particular risk because in American habitats the death cap resembles the paddy-straw (*Volvariella volvacea*), a popular food in Indochina.

Death caps are up to 6 inches tall, with a cap that's 2¼ to 6 inches wide, smooth, with greenish to yellowish pigments. The gills are white and crowded together. When young the whole fungus is covered in a membranous "veil," and parts of this may still adhere to the mature fungus. The stalk is pallid or white, with a bulbous base, or *volva*, which may be hidden beneath the soil. It grows in woodlands and flourishes between October and December.

The main toxins are phalloidin, a phallotoxin, and alpha-amanitin, an amatoxin. Phalloidin is not well absorbed into the body but does bind to the muscle cells in the gut walls, combining with one of the muscle proteins and affecting gut motility. Amanitin is a smaller molecule and is absorbed into the bloodstream, making its way to the liver where it has a strong affinity for liver cells, where it disrupts the process of making proteins and slowly kills the cells.

Symptoms

The symptoms of phalloidin poisoning are felt first. Within around 12 hours of ingestion there is violent, bloody diarrhea, together with stomach pain and vomiting. These symptoms may improve, and are often mistaken for gastric virus or flu, but within about three days the effect on the liver is felt. Liver damage causes jaundice, and kidney damage also occurs. Liver damage is progressive and can eventually cause coma and death.

Treatment

In the past, if mushroom poisoning was suspected immediately the traditional response was the use of emetics, but this is no longer the first resort. Early diagnosis of amatoxin poisoning allows the use of milk-thistle extract, which contains active flavonoids including silymarin, which inhibit amatoxin toxicity. This may be accompanied by blood dialysis. If the toxicity is not caught early enough, liver damage will be too severe and a transplant will be the only option.

Ergot

Overview Medieval Europe lived in terror of a horrific epidemic that might strike entire populations, afflicting them with St. Anthony's Fire—burning, blackening, and gangrene of the limbs—and St. Vitus's Dance—painful convulsions, accompanied by hallucinations. An outbreak known as the Plague of Fire is believed to have killed up to 40,000 people in tenth-century France, and it has reoccurred sporadically in Europe up to the present day, including La Grande Peur of France in 1789, when rioting peasants seemed crazed and psychotic.

It is now thought that these outbreaks were due to the ergot mold, which affects rye and other grains—it causes a reddish discoloration of flour, which is less visible with dark rye flour. The mold, mainly caused by *Claviceps purpurea*, causes a black spur to grow on the rye stalk, and this resembles a cock's spur, or *ergot* in French.

Symptoms Ergot alkaloids have two main effects. One is constriction of small blood vessels, which leads to circulatory problems and gangrene in the extremities. Initial symptoms would be itchiness, leading to burning sensation and necrosis, with blackening of the flesh. The other class of symptoms are caused by the convulsive and hallucinogenic effects of ergotamine, which is a precursor in the synthesis of LSD and has similar psychoactive effects. Vivid hallucinations, for instance of fierce animals or blood running down the walls, are accompanied by severe convulsions. It has been suggested that the witchcraft panic of Salem, Massachusetts, in 1691 was triggered by an outbreak of ergotism.

Treatment There is no specific antidote, but the gangrenous symptoms are treated with vasodilators and anticoagulants, while diazepam is given for convulsive symptoms and sedation for hallucinations. Ergot alkaloids have useful medical properties, such as controlling post-partum bleeding.

Source:
Claviceps purpurea and other *Claviceps* species

Form:
Mold affecting rye and other crops; active ingredients include ergotamine and other ergot alkaloids

Antidote:
None

Famous Cases

Plague of Fire,
France
(944)

Salem witch-trials
(1691)

La Grande Peur,
France
(1789)

POISONOUS ELEMENTS

There are about 80 elements in the Earth's crust, and all of them are present in the human body in varying quantities. Some 25 of these are essential to the body's structure and function, but some are only needed in minute quantities, and in anything more than trace amounts they can be toxic. There are four elements in particular—mercury, arsenic, lead, and antimony—that are probably not essential and can in fact be very highly toxic, but can be detected in even the healthiest human body. Moreover, as the familiarity of their names suggests, they play an important role in the history of poisoning.

Because of their potent effects on human physiology, these elements have long been given in one form or another as medicines, and they have also been important in the manufacture of cosmetics and dyes, as well as in other industries. This usefulness has often brought these deadly elements into unhealthily close contact with humans, a proximity which has resulted in an accumulated wealth of folklore, superstition, and strange and evocative names, from calomel to corrosive sublimate.

Perpetual Pills and Gray Powder

Now that the toxic properties of these elements are widely known it seems bizarre, but for most of recorded history people have been eagerly dosing themselves with mercury, arsenic, lead, and antimony, with physicians and industrialists acting as cheerleaders. The ancient Egyptian Ebers Papyrus (see p. 71)—one of the oldest medical texts in existence—recommended the use of stibnite (black antimony sulfide) for fevers and skin conditions, while mercury still featured in most national pharmacopoeias as late as the 1970s. Popular forms included the "blue pill"—a ball of mercury mixed with sugar that was used as a laxative—and the "perpetual pill"—a pellet of antimony that would irritate the gut and act as a purgative. As its name suggests, the pill itself was left unscathed by its passage and would be retrieved from the excrement, washed, and reused. Perpetual pills were even handed down within families from one generation to the next.

Mercury became particularly important in the late fifeenth century as a treatment for syphilis, in the form of gray powder—a mix of mercury and chalk—and later Paracelsus was a vocal advocate for its use. He made pills from red mercury oxide and cherry juice, and bathed venereal ulcers in solutions of corrosive sublimate and lime water. Mercury was in fact an effective treatment for syphilis, in that it killed the parasitic organism that caused the disease (see p. 29), but the patient also suffered. The most important antimony medicines were James's Powder, patented by British physician Robert James in 1747 and used for the next century and a half to treat fevers; and tartar emetic (potassium antimony tartrate), first described in 1631 and still in use in the late nineteenth century. The latter was prescribed for fevers because it stimulated sweating, and employed in larger doses as an emetic (to encourage vomiting). Arsenic was also an important medicine from ancient times (see pp. 84–9), while lead was ubiquitous in Roman times (see pp. 75–7).

Alchemists and Industrialists

All four of the main toxic elements are still important in the world economy. Antimony is used as an additive for glass, ceramics, lead shot, and semiconductors; lead is used in ammunition, car batteries, and television screens; mercury is important in the chemical industry; and even arsenic is still used for semiconductors, wood preservatives, and animal feed additives.

In the past, however, these deadly elements were used even more extensively. Lead has been used in plumbing, petrol additives, wine additives, solder, hair dye, and eye liner. Antimony has been used as a fire-retardant, fixing agent for dyes, and metal additive for alloys. Meanwhile arsenic (see pp. 84–9 was extensively used for dyes and colorings—for example, in wallpapers—and for pesticides, such as rat poison, and it was in this guise that most murderers obtained their deadly weapon. Mercury was, and still is, important for gold production, while it used to be a catalyst for several processes in industrial chemistry,

MERCURY

Source:
Mercury ores, such as cinnabar

Form:
Elemental mercury is silver metallic liquid at room temperature; compounds vary in properties

Antidote:
Dimercaprol

Overview Long regarded as having almost magical properties in its elemental form, mercury was also one of the most important ingredients in the pre-modern pharmacopoeia. Its toxicity varies greatly depending on its form. Liquid mercury is remarkably non-toxic for a poisonous element, because it is not well absorbed by the gut. It can be swallowed with a low risk of danger, and there are even cases where people have injected themselves and survived. Mercury vapor is much more easily absorbed through the lungs, and is therefore much more toxic. The most toxic form is organic mercury, which is very easily absorbed and easily crosses the blood–brain barrier.

Symptoms In very acute cases, death can occur within a few days, with damage to internal organs and the mouth and generic symptoms such as vomiting, weak pulse, and respiratory distress. In less acute and chronic poisoning, one of the first symptoms to appear is excessive salivation. Mercury continues to attack the mouth, causing a foul odor, inflammation of the lips, gums, and teeth—which become covered with a grey film—and eventually loss of teeth and gum tissue. Mercury affects the kidneys, initially acting as a diuretic, stimulating the flow of urine, but eventually damaging the kidneys so much that they cannot function. Mercury particularly affects the central nervous system, causing tremors and shaking—sometimes evidenced by the telltale spidery handwriting of chronic mercury poisoning sufferers. This leads on to mental deterioration, traditionally known as erethism, symptoms of which include mood swings between timidity and irritability and outbursts of anger, poor concentration, depression, memory problems, apathy, insomnia, and paranoia.

Treatment Chelating agents—chemicals that bind to metals so that they can more easily be filtered out of the blood by the kidneys, or in extreme cases by dialysis—are available, such as dimercaprol.

FAMOUS CASES

Isaac Newton
(1643–1727)

Charles II
(1630–85)

Sir Thomas Overbury
(1581–1613)

Minamata Bay
(1950s and '60s)

which has caused some serious outbreaks of industrial poisoning, notably the Minamata Bay tragedy.

From 1932 to 1968 pollution from a chemical works in Minamata Bay in Japan was discharged into the sea. Mercury oxide—which had been used as a catalyst for the production of vinyl chloride and acetaldehyde—from the effluent settled into the seafloor sediment, where it was metabolized by bacteria that transformed it into organic methyl mercury. This passed up the food chain into the fish that formed the basis of the Bay's economy and diet. The first signs of impending disaster were dead fish and affected seabirds. Then the town's cats began to stagger, salivate heavily, and die. By 1956 the people of the area began to be afflicted with what was known as *kibyo*, or "mystery disease," which had a frightening death rate of up to 40 percent. In 1958 this was diagnozed as methyl mercury poisoning, but outbreaks continued to kill dozens and cause widespread congenital disorders, such as cerebral palsy, for some time afterwards.

An earlier example of occupational mercury poisoning lives on in the phrase "mad as a hatter." As flippantly as the idiom is now employed, mercury nitrate once posed a very real risk to those in the hat-making process. Up to 40 percent of fur cutters were afflicted with chronic mercury poisoning, displaying symptoms such as irritability, paranoia, and bizarre behavior.

Almost as infamous was "phossy jaw"—one of the most grotesque examples of industrial poisoning—a condition that afflicted workers in factories making phosphorus matches. In the process of manufacture phosphorus became deposited in the jawbone, causing abscesses and tissue death with foul-smelling discharges, brain damage, and eventually death. Sufferers' jaws would even take on the eerie luminous properties of the element itself.

Charles II and the Alchemists

Aside from its more prosaic applications, mercury was also the favorite tool of alchemists, who believed it had mystical properties because it was the only liquid metal and could dissolve other metals. In the course of their research, many alchemists would have unwittingly exposed themselves to mercury vapor—which is odorless—with toxic consequences. One notable example was the great scientist Sir Isaac Newton, a keen alchemist who experimented extensively with mercury. In 1693 he had an unexplained mental breakdown, in the course of which he displayed paranoia and confused thinking, and complained of insomnia and upset digestion. These are typical symptoms of mercury poisoning, and a twentieth-century analysis of strands of hair believed to have belonged to him showed very high levels of the metal—although he lived to a ripe old age and retained his intellectual powers into his eighties. Perhaps Newton's bout of apparent psychosis was linked with an episode of acute exposure to mercury vapors.

Even royalty dabbled in "chymistry," and King Charles II of England had a particular interest in alchemy because he was perennially in need of money—the object of most alchemical research being to turn base metals into gold. He had a laboratory built in the basement of the Palace of Westminster, described by the diarist Samuel Pepys as "a pretty place," in which he saw "a great many Chymicall glasses and things, but understood none of them." The king and his assistants worked with cinnabar (mercury ore) and with the metal itself. In fact, Charles was said to be obsessed with "fixing" mercury, which meant combining it with other substances, and involved large-scale heating of liquid mercury. Like many alchemical adventurers he would have been heavily exposed to mercury vapor on a chronic basis, and it seems very likely that he was killed by an acute bout of mercury poisoning.

Noted for his cheerful disposition, the king first displayed signs of chronic mercury poisoning in 1684, becoming irritable and moody. At the end of January 1685 there was almost certainly an incident in his laboratory that caused a heavy exposure to mercury fumes, because on February 2 his health took an abrupt turn for the worse.

The Calendar of State Papers recorded that: "When his Majesty arose yesterday morning, he complained that he was not well and it was perceived by those in his chamber that he faltered somewhat in his speech." After visiting his closet "he was taken with a fit of apoplexy and convulsions," and went on to have three more fits and display stroke-like symptoms. All the trials of seventeenth-century medicine were visited upon him, with cupping, blistering, emetics, and enemas, and the next morning he seemed to have gone into remission; but over the next few days he relapsed, suffering more convulsions and weakening fast. Extreme remedies such as an extract of human skull and the application of a bezoar (see p. 30) could not save him, and he died around noon on Friday, February 6, 1685.

The Case Against Mercury

The theory that Charles was killed by mercury poisoning has been advanced by a number of sources, from romantic novelist Barbara Cartland to Frederick Holmes, a professor of medicine. Analysis of a sample of Charles's hair carried out in the twentieth century showed levels of mercury ten times higher than normal, suggesting that he was indeed exposed to chronic mercury poisoning. However, Holmes points out that the definitive evidence of acute poisoning comes from the seventeenth century itself. The autopsy carried out on the dead monarch showed distinctive changes to his brain, which would explain the epileptic symptoms he suffered. His other organs remained unaffected, but the ventricles and the tissues of the brain were soaked in serous matter, showing that serum—the protein-containing part of the blood—had leaked across the blood–brain barrier into the cerebrospinal fluid.

According to Holmes, the only cause that could account for these findings was acute mercury poisoning caused by the inhalation of a large amount of vapor at one time. Entering the bloodstream via the lungs, a huge dose of mercury would be carried directly to the brain where it would damage the integrity of the blood–brain barrier, allowing serum to contaminate the cerebrospinal fluid. Once in the brain the mercury then attacked its cells, causing the neurological symptoms that Charles displayed. And as the king died before his other organs were affected, it is suggested he must have inhaled a very large dose indeed. Like many other alchemists, Charles II's quest for gold had led him not to untold riches, but instead to a grisly death at the hands of a poisonous element.

A 1910 M. L. Kirk illustration of the Mad Hatter's tea party, in *Alice's Adventures in Wonderland*, in which the eponymous host displays classic symptoms of the mercury poisoning that afflicted so many in his profession.

CHAPTER THREE

POISON

IN

HISTORY

"The atrocious system of poisoning has been practised in all ages."

Charles Mackay (1814–89), *Memoirs of Extraordinary Popular Delusions and the Madness of Crowds*

POISON AND POISONING HAVE A LONG AND IGNOBLE HISTORY. POISONS ARE MENTIONED IN THE GREAT EPICS OF THE ANCIENT WORLD, FROM *GILGAMESH* AND HOMER, TO THE BIBLE AND THE *RAMAYANA*. POISONS HAVE LAID KINGS LOW AND RAISED UP EMPERORS, TURNED BACK ARMIES AND BROUGHT DOWN EMPIRES, BUT THE HISTORY OF POISON IS ALSO THE HISTORY OF MEDICINE, AND ALSO A SIGNIFICANT PART OF THE HISTORIES OF SCIENCE, INDUSTRY, AND AGRICULTURE.

The history of poison probably predates humanity, for as discussed in the previous chapter certain animal species seem to have some awareness of botanical pharmacology, and can make use of plant poisons. More generally, many animals know to avoid toxic plants or animals, so it can be assumed that early hominids would have shared some degree of innate knowledge, expanded upon by the bitter experience of trial and error.

To understand properly just how sophisticated the knowledge and use of natural toxins was in prehistoric times, we need to look to the nearest contemporary analogs in the form of pre-industrial cultures, such as Amazonian Indians, Kalahari nomads, and New Guinean tribespeople. People from these cultures, particularly shamans and medicine men, often hold vast mental databases of the toxic and therapeutic properties of their habitats, and it is reasonable to assume that prehistoric men and women shared a similar knowledge of their world. Inevitably, little evidence of this has survived the passage of time, but there are some clues from archeology and ancient traditions that allow the first pages of the history of poison to be written.

Poison In the Ancient World

Given that there is evidence for the use of poisons in prehistory, it is hardly surprising that they should be found in humanity's early texts. In fact, arrow poisons—the term "toxin" derives from the ancient Greek *toxikon*, meaning "arrow poison"—are mentioned in the Bible, and in Homer, where Odysseus makes a special voyage to obtain "a deadly drug that he might have wherewithal to smear his bronze-shod arrows." The ancient Celts used hellebore juice as an arrow poison, while the ancient Chinese used aconite, which was also used in Europe to kill wolves, hence its alternative name, wolfsbane.

Arrow poison has also been used by both North American and African peoples. Often it was believed that letting the poison "brew" along with putrefying animal parts and plant matter would enhance its strength, although the opposite was probably true. For instance, Native Americans would obtain venom by getting a snake to bite the liver of a deer, and then allow this to putrefy along with toxic leaves; while in Africa, puff-adder heads were allowed to marinate with resin, beetles, and toxic leaves—although probably more effective was the practice of Kalahari people who mixed the venom of a spitting cobra with resin to produce a toxic gum used to coat their arrow tips.

In South America the equivalent practice was the use of poisonous frogs, which were induced to "sweat" the poison from their backs. One of the first Westerners to record this practice was the intrepid British sailor Captain Charles Cochrane. In 1824 he saw the practice in Colombia, describing how the natives stored the frogs in hollow canes until they were required:

> *"they take out one of the unfortunate reptiles and pass a pointed piece of wood down its throat, and out of one of his legs. This torture makes the poor frog perspire very much, especially on the back, which becomes covered with white froth; this is the most powerful poison that he yields, and in this they dip or roll the points of their arrows, which will preserve their destructive power for a year."*

Another method practiced since prehistoric times is the use of pisci-cides—poisons particularly toxic to fish, which stun or kill fish so that they can easily be recovered. The ancient roots of the practice are attested by archeo-logical discoveries from the Engoroy Culture, an Ecuadorian culture of the first millennium, showing the use of the piscicide *Jacquinia sprucei*.

Ancient Medicine

The first hard evidence of the true study of poisons, or toxicology, comes through the practice of medicine. In ancient Egyptian tombs, traces of such plant poisons as opium and cannabis have been found, probably because they were important medicines; and the most ancient medical texts record extensive thera-peutic use of poisons. Sumerian and Akkadian texts record knowledge of poisonous plants such as black nightshade and spurge, and recommend treat-ments for bites and stings from spiders and scorpions. They even emphasize the use of vinegar to detoxify poisons, a practice continued for thousands of years. In fact, one of the deities in the ancient Mesopotamian pantheon was Gula, who was specifically invoked in matters of poisoning.

The Ebers Papyrus, which dates from 1534 BC, although parts are much older, is rich in references to poison, and shows that the ancient Egyptians were familiar with hemlock, aconite, opium, lead, antimony, and possibly even ricin, digitalis, and belladonna. That said, scorpion and snake venoms were mainly treated with charms, spells, and prayers, so Egyptian toxicology clearly had its limits. Then, a few centuries later, ancient Indian texts included the *samhita* (medical treatise) of the sixth-century BC physician Susruta, which offered advice ranging from how to avoid contamination of food, to music therapy—drum beats were said to have antivenomous virtues.

However, according to Chinese tradition, both ancient Egyptian and Indian sources are predated by Shen Nung, the legendary father of Chinese med-icine. His *Pen Ts'ao Ching* supposedly dates back to 2696 BC, and lists 365 natural medicines, including many mineral, plant, and animal poisons. However, like many toxicologists Shen Nung is said to have fallen foul of the subject of his study after tasting one toxic herb too many.

The Greek and Roman Era

Greek myths and legends, and the works of Homer, attest to a long history of knowledge and use of poisons in Europe, but the Greeks and Romans associated poison with the corrupt and decadent East, or regarded it as the preserve of murderers and assassins. The kingdom of Pontus, for instance, was notorious for the availability of poisons and their use in political intrigues.

In his *Metamorphoses* of around AD 8, Ovid reflected the Roman view of such antics, lamenting that since humankind's fall from the Golden Age, "The husband longed for the death of his wife, she of her husband; murderous step-mothers brewed deadly poisons, and sons inquired into their fathers' years before the time." But he was also passing comment on his own era, for the use of poisons to dispose of inconvenient husbands had grown to such epidemic pro-portions in the republican period that in 82 BC the dictator Sulla was forced to pass a specific law, the *Lex Cornelia de sicariis et veneficis* ("concerning assassins and sorcerers"), in which were set out punishments for those who employed poison, but also for those who made, sold, bought, possessed, or gave poison for the purpose of murder. However, even this failed to discourage the leading women of the imperial era (see pp. 116–19).

Meanwhile, toxicology had also made advances. Hippocrates, the Greek father of medicine, who lived around 400 BC, was one of the first to approach the treatment of poisons rationally and systematically. He added more poisons to the pharmacopoeia, introduced concepts of bioavailability via his understanding of the need to limit absorption of In the gut, and discussed the concept of the overdose. He was followed by great physicians such as Theophrastus (370–286 BC), who listed poisonous plants in his *De Historia Plantarum*, and Nicander of Colophon (185–135 BC), who apparently experimented on criminals in compos-ing a treatise on antidotes that discussed poisons such as ceruse (white lead), litharge (red lead oxide), aconite, cantharides, conium (hemlock), hyoscamus (henbane), and opium.

Dioscorides, a Greek physician at the court of the emperor Nero, authored an influential *Materia Medica* in 65 CE, which was among the first works to classify poisons as animal, vegetable, or mineral—a typology still useful today. This work remained a standard reference for the next 16 centuries, and was among the first to record the use of emetics, the standard treatment for ingested poisons until very recently (see p. 31). Therapeutic poisons and the science of antidotes also featured in the Greek physician Galen's second-century works, which formed the basis of Western medicine until the Enlightenment.

Hercules and the Cloak of Nessus

Reflecting this classical obsession with poisons is the story of Hercules, the greatest of all the Greek heroes. For example, the twelfth of his famous labors, the task of retrieving Cerberus from Hades, was said to have engendered the deadly herb aconite, or wolfsbane. Ovid's *Metamorphoses* relates that:

> "The dog struggled, twisting its head away from the daylight and the shining sun. Mad with rage, it filled the air with its triple barking, and sprinkled the green fields with flecks of white foam. These flecks are thought to have taken root and, finding nourishment in the rich and fertile soil, acquired harmful properties. Since they flourish on hard rock, the country folk call them aconites, rock-flowers."

Hercules' second labor had been the destruction of the Lernean Hydra, a terrible many-headed serpent monster, offspring of Echidna, "Mother of All Monsters," which was so poisonous that its bite, blood, and even breath were deadly. After he successfully overcame the beast—thanks to some quick thinking on the part of his companion, Iolaus, who cauterized the stumps of its severed heads so that they could not grow back, and a heavy rock, with which he immobilized the Hydra's remaining, immortal, head—Hercules dipped his arrows into its blood, thus creating what classical folklorist Adrienne Mayor describes as the first biological weapon in Western literature. However, Hercules' poison arrows proved double-edged. Although they helped him to slay innumerable enemies, including an entire horde of enraged centaurs, they also claimed the lives of friends

and allies such as the wise centaur Chiron. Inquisitive to examine one of Hercules' arrows, Chiron scratched his foot in doing so and died instantly, arguably becoming the first in a long line of toxicologists killed by the object of their study.

Subsequently, Hercules tangled with another centaur, Nessus. Catching Nessus attempting to take liberties with his wife, Deianira, Hercules shot him with two poisoned arrows, but even as he died the centaur hatched a plan for revenge. With his dying breath he told Deianira that his blood-soaked cloak would help to ensure that Hercules would remain faithful to her, but what she didn't realize was that the centaur's blood was now contaminated with the deadly poison. Years later when she feared the hero was bestowing his favors upon another, she sent him the cloak, and Hercules slipped it on with horrific consequences: as Ovid relates it "ripped his skin from his burning flesh. As his great strength pulled, it stripped the great muscles from his limbs, leaving his huge bones bare. Even his blood audibly hissed... "

After his demise, Hercules' arrows passed to Philoctetes, who used them to good effect in the Trojan War—his victims including the Trojan prince Paris, who was denied the antidote by his vengeful wife—but later retired them by depositing them at a temple to Apollo, god of healing.

Did Lead Bring Down the Roman Empire?

The theory that chronic epidemic lead poisoning may have played a role in the decline of the Roman Empire was first advanced in 1965 by S. C. Gilfillan, who claimed that "lead poisoning is to be reckoned the major influence in the ruin of the Roman culture, progressiveness, and genius." Although comprehensively dismantled at the time, this theory was revived in 1983 by geochemist Jerome Nriagu in the *New England Journal of Medicine*, and subsequently in his book *Lead and Lead Poisoning in Antiquity*.

Hercules Vanquishing the Hydra (1620–1) by Guido Reni. The hydra was a monster so poisonous that even its breath was lethal, while its blood retained its toxicity indefinitely, eventually accounting for Hercules' death many years later.

The crux of the lead argument is that the ancient Romans, and in particular the Roman aristocracy, were exposed to high levels of lead through the water and wine they drank, the food they ate, and the make-up and medicines they applied. The Roman era marked the start of large-scale industrial exploitation of lead, partly as a by-product of silver mining, but also because it is one of the most easily recovered, easily worked, and useful metals available. Lead can be melted on a camp fire, worked easily into sheets and pipes, and is resistant to rusting and erosion. Alloyed with tin it could be used to make pewter for dishes and drinking vessels. As white lead, or ceruse, it made a striking paint or cosmetic, which the Romans used, along with other forms, in wall paint, make-up, hair dye, fillings, and medicine.

Lead was mined in Greece, Spain, Britain, and Sardinia, with production in excess of 100,000 tons a year. Proxy records from ice cores and peat bogs show that atmospheric contamination caused by lead rocketed fourfold around the time.

The Romans were justly famous for their feats of hydrological engineering, and lead pipes were a key part of this, but water thus conveyed would dissolve some of the lead. Did the Romans show signs of lead poisoning, known to the Romans as plumbism or saturnism? Well, many emperors displayed mental health problems and gout, both symptomatic of lead poisoning, while the ruling classes were noted for their low fertility and birth rate, which could also be symptoms. Chronic ill health and low fertility amongst the ruling elite, Nriagu suggests, lay behind the decline of the empire.

The Case Against Plumbism

Most of these points have been challenged strongly. The Romans were well aware of the dangers of lead poisoning, which was described by classical authorities such as Nicander, so shouldn't they have noticed epidemic plumbism? And, in any case, how much did they really ingest?

The Romans knew that lead water pipes were dangerous, and that terracotta was much more desirable—"Water conducted through earthen pipes is more wholesome than that through lead; indeed that conveyed in lead must be injurious, because from it white lead is obtained, and this is said to be injurious to the human system," wrote the Augustan architect Vitruvius. Also, calcium carbonate in the water of Rome meant that deposits quickly built up on the inside of water pipes, so that they had to be cleaned frequently, and this would have prevented lead from leaching into the water.

Sapa, a sweetening agent manufactured in lead pans, was a more serious problem, but this was added to wine in small amounts, and then the wine itself was diluted with water. Also, it may be that although lead pans were considered best for sapa production, bronze pans were more often used. When lead pans were used, they may have been extremely big, thus reducing the ratio of the surface area of the sapa-pan to the volume of sapa.

Then comes the question of the low birth rate among the aristocracy; but this can be easily explained without invoking lead. In fact, the Romans themselves recognized only too well that being childless could be fun: "so powerful were the attractions of a childless state... that many were actively choosing not to marry or have children," wrote Tacitus in the early second century CE. Augustus, the first emperor, was sufficiently worried that he enacted laws to promote marriage and procreation, and this was long before Rome's grasp on the ancient world began to loosen. On balance, while the Romans may well have been exposed to unhealthy levels of lead, it seems quite unlikely that it played a crucial part in their downfall.

Rainwater, which is slightly acidic, can pick up lead from roofs and pipes—the one shown dates from c. 161–180 AD—as much as 1 mg per liter. But much higher levels would have come from sapa (see above). In either case, only a few percent of ingested lead is absorbed by the gut, but levels of just 80 mg per 100 ml of blood can cause acute poisoning. Modern recreations of sapa suggest it could have contained up to 1,000 parts per million of lead (0.1 percent), meaning that just a single spoonful could have caused mild poisoning.

The Golden Age of Poisoning

For all that the Greeks, Romans, Persians, and other cultures of the ancient world embraced the use of poison, it was in Renaissance Europe that the poisoners' art truly flowered. In an age supposedly characterized by humanism and enlightenment, chemical murder and assassination were rife. Competition between city-states drove the evolution of sophisticated systems of diplomacy, finance, politics, and war, and poison appealed to all these domains. The records of city councils in Florence and Siena, for instance, show how victims were selected, and assassins contracted and paid, but it was in Venice that the practice was most infamous. The Council of Ten, a special tribunal created to co-ordinate "black ops," recorded its nefarious transactions in a ledger marked *Secreto Secretissima*—"Top Top Secret"—which still sits in the city's archives. Anyone who displeased the Council was marked for death, and foreign assassins were contracted to poison them, presumably in order to ensure full deniability.

The Gift of the Borgias

Much better known are the dark deeds of the Borgias, the family who clawed their way to power in Rome in the late fifteenth century. Rodrigo Borgia became Pope Alexander VI in 1492, and together with his illegitimate son Cesare, has since been accused of all manner of infamy. The Borgias were renowned for asking to dinner anyone who posed an obstacle to them. Then they would take advantage of the highly spiced nature of contemporary cuisine to mask the taste of deadly poison, and were even said to maintain a cadre of Italian astrologer-chemists who would concoct toxic brews from mercury, arsenic, aconite, yew, henbane, phosphorus, hemlock, and poppy.

A favorite Borgia poison was *la cantarella*, a slightly sweet white powder that could be slipped into wine or food. It is thought to have been a combination of arsenic, phosphorus, and lead acetate, also known as lead sugar. In addition

Cesare had a poison-dispensing ring fashioned in the shape of a lion's head with two sharp "fangs" on the bottom, so that he could prick his victims with a handshake. Meanwhile, his father, for his part, would ask guests to the papal apartments to unlock a particular cabinet for him—the key was stiff, and equipped with a poison-tipped pin on the handle that would puncture the victim's flesh when he pressed on it.

According to a story repeated by Michel de Montaigne and others, the Borgias eventually undid themselves. Cesare resolved to poison the cardinal of Corneto, and accordingly invited him for dinner in the Vatican. He sent a poisoned bottle of wine to the Pope's butler with instructions to take special care of it. When Alexander arrived early and called for fine wine, the butler assumed that Cesare's bottle must be of special quality and served it. Cesare arrived not long after and, assuming that whatever his father was drinking must be alright, joined him. The Pope died almost immediately but Cesare, young and robust, survived despite suffering terrible agonies. "Can there be a more express act of justice than this?" wondered Montaigne.

The Young Widows' Poisoning Club

A plague of poisoning descended on Italy in the century that followed. In his classic 1841 work *Memoirs of Extraordinary Popular Delusions and the Madness of Crowds*, Charles Mackay recounts the history of a group of young Roman wives who, perhaps inspired by their ancient forebears, took to poisoning their husbands so that they could enjoy life as merry widows. The epidemic of mariticide only came to light in 1659 when the mass of malefactors unburdening themselves to their confessors led the Pope to instigate an investigation. The supplier of the femmes fatales, proved to be, in the words of Mackay, a "hag [and] reputed witch and fortune-teller" named Hieronyma Spara, who dispensed "a slow poison—clear, tasteless and limpid" that was marketed as *aquetta di Perugia*.

La Spara was tortured and put to death—although the murderesses themselves, thanks to their higher social status, got away with whipping or banishment—but her baton was taken up almost immediately by another woman, Tophania of Naples. The arsenical poison she sold became famous as *aqua di Toffana*, and allegedly came complete with a set of instructions for disposing of inconvenient relatives—just four drops were enough to kill. However, in 1719 Tophania too was captured and executed.

By this time what Mackay calls "the mania for poisoning" had already taken root in France, supposedly transmitted there by the sixteenth-century Italian princess Catherine de Medici, who was accused of every sort of infamy by her enemies. Her list of alleged victims includes her husband's older brother, the heir to the throne, and the cardinal of Lorraine. It was even said that she made the word *italien* synonymous with *empoisonneur*.

One of Catherine's enemies, Jean of Navarre, was supposedly murdered by a poisoner named René the Florentine, who sold her a pair of gloves laced with *venin de crapaud*, a contender for the accolade of most unpleasant poison ever: it was made by feeding arsenic to toads, leaving them to decompose, and then bottling the foul juices that leaked out.

Catherine is often accused of being the first experimental toxicologist—although this seems unlikely, considering, for example, similar claims made about Cleopatra (see pp. 175–8)—thanks to her alleged practice of testing various poisons on the poor and sick, under the disguise of dispensing medicine. Supposedly she would deliberately start off with sub-lethal doses in order to observe their effects, and then increase the amounts until she found the lethal dose.

However, it is telling that exactly the same story is told of Madame de Brinvilliers, protagonist of the sordid Affaire des Poisons (see pp. 144–6). Together with an alleged witch Catherine Deshayes, also known as la Voisin, she was accused of using and supplying arsenical poisons, often known as *poudres de succession*, because of their use by those impatient for their inheritance. Arsenic was so prevalent that this period became known as "the age of arsenic."

The Birth of Toxicology

After the collapse of Rome, the torch of learning passed to the Islamic world, which produced works such as Jabir's ninth-century CE *Kitab al-sumum—Book of Poisons*—the chapters of which dealt with In the body, In the natural world, specific symptoms, venomous animals, and antidotes and remedies. It even included recipes for unwholesome brews: "Take a gecko and a yellow tarantula, then pulverize them both finely; they are mixed with milk and left to ferment."

The next significant toxicologist in the West was Moses Maimonides (1135–1204), a Jewish physician from Muslim Spain whose works included *Poisons and Their Antidotes* (1198). Like Hippocrates he was aware of the need to limit bioavailability, noting that milk, butter, and cream acted to delay intestinal absorption of poisons. He also recommended the use of tourniquets to prevent venom from a bite spreading to the rest of the body.

The true foundation of toxicology, however, is usually traced to the work of Theophrastus von Hohenheim (1493–1541), better known as Paracelsus. A Swiss-German physician, alchemist, and natural philosopher, Paracelsus was notorious for his revolutionary views on medicine and many other topics. He emphasized the importance of experiment, appreciated that specific chemicals had specific effects—including toxicity—distinguished between the therapeutic and toxic properties, and elucidated the relationship between dosage and response.

At this time other natural philosophers were also making links between substances and their toxic effects. Around 1480 Ellenborg warned of the dangers of mercury and lead for goldsmiths. Then, in 1556, Agricola wrote a treatise on mining that included investigation of occupational toxicology, which was followed in 1567 by a posthumously published treatise penned by Paracelsus himself: *On the Miners' Sickness and Other Diseases of Miners.*

The Poison Detectives

This growing understanding of the nature and mechanism of toxins was reflected in both medicine and crime, as murderers increasingly took advantage of new poisons—mostly those marketed as pesticides or medicines—safe in the knowledge that there was little chance of being detected.

This was to change with the development of forensic toxicology, the science of detection of poisons. In 1832 British chemist James Marsh was asked to analyze human remains and leftover coffee, in an attempt to prove the guilt of

John Bodle, suspected of having poisoned his grandfather to gain an inheritance. A pharmacist testified that he had sold Bodle white arsenic (arsenic trioxide)—the favorite tool of the poisoner—and Marsh used a standard test to show the presence of arsenic in the old man's organs, and in some coffee he had been given by his grandson. Bubbling hydrogen sulfide gas through a solution made from the suspect materials, Marsh obtained the telltale yellow precipitate of arsenic sulfide. But by the time the case came to trial, the samples had discolored and the jury let Bodle go free.

Angered by this travesty of justice, Marsh set about perfecting a new test for arsenic, in which the target tissue was heated and dissolved with acid. Adding zinc to the acid converted the arsenic into arsine gas (AsH_3), which was passed through a heated tube. The gas would break down and metallic arsenic would be deposited in a thin film, and measured. The Marsh test was so effective it could detect as little as 0.02 mg of arsenic in a sample.

The first man to use the Marsh test to secure a conviction was pioneering toxicologist Mathieu Orfila, a Spanish physician based in Paris and author of a seminal 1814 work called *Traité des Poisons ou Toxicologie Générale*—the fruit of research that cost the lives of 4,000 dogs. Called to testify in the 1839 trial of Madame LeFarge, an unhappy wife accused of poisoning her husband after being seen mixing a white powder into his drink while nursing him during a fatal "illness," Orfila was able to show the presence of arsenic in Monsieur LeFarge's body. Madame was sentenced to life imprisonment.

During the nineteenth and early twentieth centuries, tests for almost all known poisons were developed, including a test for alkaloids, which covers most plant poisons, in 1851. Thanks to modern methods, such as chromatography, mass spectroscopy, and neutron activation analysis, it is no longer possible for the poisoner to act with impunity. In fact, with rare exceptions, poisoners can be sure that if foul play is suspected, the murder weapon will inevitably be detected.

An engraved portrait of Paracelsus from the 1567 book *Astronomica et Astrologica*, showing him clutching a sword pommel bearing the legend "Zoth," possibly a form of "Azoth," one of the alchemical names for mercury.

ARSENIC, THE KING OF POISONS

Although we have touched upon toxic elements already (see pp. 59–63), arsenic occupies a special place in the history of poisons. For several centuries from the Middle Ages up to modern times it was the poison of choice for murderers. Easily made by chemists and as a by-product of industrial processes, arsenic was cheap and widely available, mainly as a poison for rats and other vermin, but also in medicines and other forms. The most common form, white arsenic or arsenic trioxide, was a white powder similar in appearance to sugar, which could be added to food or drink without odor or discoloration, imparting at most a slightly sweet taste. The effects it produced were largely generic and could easily be mistaken for cholera or other common and widely feared diseases, at a time when mortality rates were much higher than they are now and it was normal for death by vomiting, diarrhea, intestinal distress, dehydration, and shock to strike without warning. Arsenic was thus easy to obtain, easy to administer, and easy to conceal.

Elemental arsenic was first isolated by thirteenth-century magus Albertus Magnus; but it had been known through its ores—realgar and orpiment—for thousands of years before. Indeed, the earliest known case of mild chronic arsenic poisoning dates back to Ötzi, a 5,000-year-old iceman preserved in an Alpine glacier, who showed high levels of arsenic in his hair, probably as a result of coppersmithing. Ancient Romans, Indians, and Chinese knew of the potency of arsenical compounds, recommending them for use as pesticides and medicines—similar uses continued into the twentieth century.

Even before arsenic was isolated in its elemental form (see box below left), arsenic in a variety of other forms has a long history as a deadly poison. For example, orpiment was known to the Assyrians of the early first millennium BC, while the Romans not only knew how to make white arsenic, but also how to make the highly soluble and thus highly toxic salt sodium arsenite. Ancient peoples of the Near and Middle East were known to make free use of poisons, while there is speculation that Sulla's famous law against poisons (see p. 72) may have been instituted as a response to rampant arsenic use. Arsenic was the weapon of choice for the lethal empress Agrippina (see pp. 116–19), and for the many femmes fatales who followed her. It was probably the active ingredient of *la cantarella, aqua di Toffana*, and *poudres de succession* (see pp. 78–80). As late as the 1930s, arsenic featured in a mini-epidemic of mariticidal poisoning, during the Great Arsenic Murder Ring of South Philadelphia, in which 24 people were found guilty of using "inheritance powders" in attempts to cash in on life-insurance policies.

Arsenic has also been an important military toxin since Byzantine times, when it was probably an ingredient of Greek Fire. During World War I the British developed arsine-derivatives called lewisite and sneeze gas, but the war was over before they could be deployed. However, lewisite was later used by the Japanese in China during World War II, and more recently still by Saddam Hussein against the Iranians in the Iraq–Iran War of the 1980s.

Fowler's Solution and Gosio's Disease

Orpiment, realgar, and other arsenical formulations had been used for medical purposes since before Hippocrates, and arsenic is still found in many Chinese medicine preparations. In the West its most popular incarnation was Fowler's solution, a recipe created by English physician Dr. Thomas Fowler after his analysis showed that other popular patent medicines contained the element. Fowler's concoction included arsenic trioxide, and a recommended dose of the potion delivered up to 5 mg of arsenic at a time. Used as a cure-all of sorts, it was prescribed for everything from epilepsy and lumbago to skin problems and syphilis.

ARSENIC

Source:
Common ores:
realgar (As_4S_4),
orpiment (As_2S_3);
mainly recovered as
by-product of copper
and lead refining

Form:
Elemental arsenic is
metallic in appearance;
most common com-
pound is white arsenic
(arsenic trioxide)—
sugarlike white powder;
also arsine gas (AsH_3)
and other compounds

Antidote:
Dimercaprol

Overview
Arsenic is a semimetallic element that binds with and disrupts sulfur-containing enzymes that are present in every cell of the body, so that it has the potential to disrupt the biochemistry of every tissue and organ in the body. It particularly targets enzymes in mitochondria, shutting off energy production, halting cell-repair mechanisms, and starving the cell. Arsine gas is toxic by a different mechanism, damaging blood cells. White arsenic, or arsenic trioxide, was the usual form in which the poison was administered, but this had consequences for the actual dose delivered. If arsenic powder was added to food, the size of the particles determined the rate of absorption. If, as was most common, it was dissolved in a drink, the delivered dose was often much less than intended because the trioxide did not dissolve well.

Symptoms
The initial reaction to an acute dose of arsenic is gastrointestinal, with diarrhea and vomiting, as well as damage to the gut lining. Severe dehydration follows, with intense thirst and soreness of mouth and throat, and stomach pains, coma, and death following within 12–36 hours. These symptoms could easily be mistaken for cholera or other diseases.

Treatment
Emesis is not recommended. Lots of fluids are needed to replace those lost through vomiting and diarrhea. Dimercaprol is the best antidote for arsenic—as a chelating agent, it competes for the arsenic ions and forms stable, soluble complexes that the kidney can easily filter out of the bloodstream. But it is only effective soon after poisoning, and can itself be toxic.

FAMOUS CASES

Claudius
(10 BC – AD 54)

Pope Alexander VI
(1437–1503)

la Voisin
(1640–80)

Napoleon Bonaparte
(1769–1821)

Mary Ann Cotton
(1832–73)

Florence Maybrick
(1862–1941)

Throughout the nineteenth century Fowler's solution was ubiquitous in every Victorian medicine chest. Charles Darwin, for instance, was known to dose himself with it regularly to treat tremor, and it may well have been the cause of both his mysterious chronic ailment and his death.

Equally ubiquitous were arsenical pigments. Orpiment and realgar had been used to make yellow and red respectively since ancient Egyptian times, and in 1775 chemist Karl Scheele made copper arsenite, a brilliant green pigment. This and another arsenic-containing pigment, emerald green, were soon in demand for everything from oil paintings, wallpapers, and linoleum dyes to candy decorations, children's toys, and soap. This led to widespread chronic exposure to arsenic and many episodes of accidental poisoning.

A particular problem was micro-organisms feasting upon wallpaper paste, and, through a mechanism suggested by Italian chemist Bartolomeo Gosio, releasing a highly toxic gas. Many people died of "Gosio's disease," even after arsenic-free dyes replaced the toxic ones at the end of the nineteenth century, and famous suspected victims of arsenical pigments include Napoleon and Clare Boothe Luce, the U.S. ambassador to Italy in the 1950s, who was nearly killed by old paint in her bedroom in the embassy in Rome.

Accidental arsenic poisoning continues to be a huge problem in many places; particularly in Bangladesh and Indian West Bengal, but also in regions of Mexico, Argentina, Mongolia, and Taiwan. In the U.S. the statutory limit for arsenic in drinking water is 50 parts per billion (ppb), but in Bangladesh levels have been found that are more than ten times this, due to arsenic in deep strata being mobilized by bacteria, carried there by water being drawn in by deep wells. Some 70 million people have been subject to chronic arsenic poisoning, many of them developing hyperkeratosis—a horny thickening of the skin—leprosy-like lesions, developmental disorders, and cancer.

The Arsenic Eaters and the Styrian Defense

In 1851 a Dr. Von Tschudi published an article in a medical journal describing the peculiar habits of peasants from the region of Styria, on the border between modern-day Austria and Hungary. People of this Alpine land claimed to eat daily doses of arsenic that would be fatal to an ordinary person, chipping bits off blocks and sprinkling it on their food like salt. Even more extraordinarily, they claimed that the arsenic was a potent tonic, giving them more "wind" for climbing, increasing endurance, improving complexion, boosting courage and libido, and benefiting health all round. They even gave it to their horses.

This strange predilection for poison traced its roots back to the seventeenth century, when mining and smelting in the region introduced the Styrians to a white deposit on the chimneys of their forges and foundries. They called it *hittrichfeitl*, or "white smoke," but it was better known as white arsenic or arsenic trioxide.

Von Tschudi's article was quickly taken up by other publications around the world and the arsenic eaters of Styria became the sensation of the Victorian medical milieu. Reports indicated that the Styrians were skilled at estimating quantities of arsenic, training themselves up from small quantities of "half a grain" (around 30 mg) taken two or three times a week to two or more grains taken daily. Some men claimed to take five grains (300 mg) daily, and to be able to tolerate even larger quantities.

Widely regarded as fanciful, these claims were dramatically put to the test at a conference in Graz, Austria, in 1875, when two Styrian peasants got up in front of a large audience and swallowed 400 mg and 300 mg respectively, reappearing the next day to prove that they were in good health. Analysis of their urine showed that much of the arsenic was safely excreted via the kidneys.

How was this possible? Clearly some degree of tolerance had been developed by gradually increasing exposure (recalling the exploits of Mithridates—see p. 33), but it is also likely that the comparatively coarse grains of white arsenic the Styrians sprinkled on food minimized the absorption of arsenic in their intestines, so that the effective delivered dose was much smaller than it appeared. It was also the case that the Styrians suffered extensive ill-effects. The plump, ruddy complexions of which they boasted were probably due to vasodilation and edema, and arsenical interference with iodine metabolism in the body also caused widespread goiters and other problems in the population.

Similarly, albeit on a smaller scale, use of arsenic for cosmetic and tonic purposes was widespread in the Victorian era, and this formed the basis for the Styrian Defense, employed by lawyers defending several prominent accused poisoners, primarily women accused of murdering their husbands with arsenic. Traces detected in the victim's body were put down to his arsenic eating—for tonic purposes—whilst the accused woman, it was explained, was in possession of arsenic for cosmetic purposes. The Styrian Defense notably featured in the trial of Florence Maybrick (see pp. 154–6).

Henry Wallis's famous painting *The Death of Chatterton*, showing the corpse of the young poet who committed suicide by drinking a preparation of arsenic in 1770.

Chapter Four

POISON

AS

EXECUTIONER

"with no rash potion,

But with a lingering dram, that should not work

Maliciously, like poison."

William Shakespeare (c. 1564–1616), *A Winter's Tale*

EXECUTING PEOPLE IS DIRTY WORK, BUT THROUGH THE USE OF POISON HUMANKIND HAS LONG SOUGHT TO WASH ITS HANDS OF THE MORE UNPALATABLE ASPECTS OF THE JOB. THERE IS A LONG HISTORY OF ATTEMPTS TO "IMPROVE" EXECUTIONS BY USING THE SPECIAL PROPERTIES OF TOXINS; WHETHER TO MAKE THE KILLING FASTER OR MORE EFFICIENT, OR TO MAKE IT LESS PAINFUL AND SUPPOSEDLY MORE HUMANE. FEW OF THESE EFFORTS HAVE MANAGED TO ACHIEVE WHAT THEY SET OUT TO DO, AND IN SEEKING TO RATIONALIZE AND MODERNIZE EXECUTION THEY HAVE MERELY SUCCEEDED IN ADDING SOME OF THE DARKEST CHAPTERS TO THE HISTORY OF POISON.

Some of the earliest recorded uses of poison for execution—and arguably the best of a very bad bunch—are from ancient Athens, and in particular from accounts of the most famous poisoned executee, the philosopher Socrates. Earlier uses can be inferred from the use of poison in some pre-modern societies (see p. 94), but the best-known use of poison for execution came more recently, in the twentieth century, when perverse notions of rationality were allied to dark motives, in the gas chambers of dictators. Although it should be noted that these too have antecedents in earlier centuries.

Today, however, the use of poisons for execution is arguably more widespread than ever before, taking the form of lethal injections. But as we shall see, even this most "modern" and apparently scientifically rationalized application of poisons is fraught with ethical and practical problems.

TRIAL BY ORDEAL

European missionaries and colonials brought back from West Africa tales of poisonous plants employed for a form of "trial by ordeal" that, like many such trials, also doubled as a method of execution for those found guilty.

Different tribes used different plants. For instance, C. J. S. Thompson, a collector and curator of medical anthropology, described the poison *muavi*: "which is used by tribes in W. Africa, prepared by scraping the bark of a poisonous tree known only to the witch-doctors. A decoction of the scrapings is made with water and the resulting draught, which is of a highly poisonous nature, is administered to the suspected person [and his accuser]." Severe vomiting and eventually death were likely to follow, but if this failed to happen with the first dose, the process was repeated until one of the parties expired. "When the guilt of one of the parties has been established by death, his property is at once confiscated and his wife and children are killed."

The Balantes tribe used sassy bark (*Erythrophlaeum guineense*), mixed with powdered glass and powdered human tissue from earlier guilty parties. Two spoonfuls of water would be added to make a paste, which could be used to test the guilt of suspected witches. Also in West Africa, the Ordeal Bean of Calabar became quite famous thanks to Scottish missionaries (see right). Similar ordeal plants were known from Madagascar—for example, the seed of the tanghin tree—and elsewhere.

One popular and plausible explanation of their efficacy is that those with a clean conscience, confident of being cleared, would quickly swallow their dose, while the guilty would furtively sip at theirs. As we have already seen (see p. 14–16), this variation in exposure could make all the difference, since while the dose ingested would be the same, the effective dose would vary according to the speed of transit of the foodstuff, and, crucially, the degree of maceration of the bean, although this only really applied where whole seeds or beans were used.

THE ORDEAL BEAN

Source:
Physostigma venenosum,
a West African vine

Form:
Bean; may be presented
as infusion of pounded
beans in water

Antidote:
None, although
atropine is used to
counteract effects

Overview When Scottish missionaries arrived in the eastern Nigerian province of Calabar in the 1840s, they discovered a widespread practice of ordeal by poisoned bean. A climbing vine of the pea family produced what the missionaries soon came to call the Ordeal Bean of Old Calabar, but which the locals called the "chop nut." Chop nuts were used to separate the innocent from the guilty and unmask witches, and in deadly duels known as *eséré*. In trials the accused would drink an infusion of pounded beans, while in duels opponents would swallow half a bean each. As with muavi (see opposite), it was said the bean was so trusted to distinguish the guilty from the innocent that people would willingly swallow the toxic preparations. According to some reports, hundreds or even thousands would gather at anti-witch rallies, swallowing beans en masse to assert their innocence. In 1846 the missionaries calculated the annual death rate by Calabar bean poisoning as around 120 per year.

The missionaries sent samples of the bean back to Scotland, where analysis revealed the presence of three active alkaloids, the main one being christened physostigmine. In 1863 there was excitement among eye doctors when it was reported that this was the first substance capable of causing constriction of the pupils, the opposite effect to atropine. This was because physostigmine is cholinergic in effect—it binds to the enzyme acetylcholinesterase and prevents it from breaking down acetylcholine, thus boosting levels of this neurotransmitter at key neuromuscular junctions. It also has a structure that allows it to cross the blood–brain barrier easily, so it strongly affects the central nervous system, including the brainstem.

Symptoms Drowsiness, pinpoint pupils, respiratory difficulty, tremor, involuntary defecation and urination, low blood pressure, seizures, irregular heartbeat, heart failure, and death from heart or breathing problems.

Treatment Atropine can counteract the effects of physostigmine. Medical applications of physostigmine include treatment for anticholinergic poisoning—for example, by atropine— triggering of ejaculation in impotent or paraplegic men, and its potential as a protective agent against nerve gas. More recently it has become one of the most effective drugs used in the treatment of Alzheimer's disease.

SOCRATES AND THE STATE POISON

One of history's earliest recorded examples of execution by poison—the death of Socrates in 399 BC—remains its most famous, partly because of the eminence of the individual involved, but also because of the many puzzles it presents. Exactly what was the nature of the poison that Socrates drank? The identity of what the Athenians called their "State Poison" is one of the great mysteries of toxicology. Why would a society famed as the birthplace of democracy and known for its regard for freedom execute a 70-year-old philosopher considered by Plato, his pupil, as "the wisest and most just of all men?" What might prompt

a jury of 500 ordinary citizens to sentence an elderly and previously respected individual to death? Socrates himself is also something of a paradox—a man who wrote nothing, and yet is one of the most influential thinkers in Western philosophy. Rather than his own works, historians must rely instead on those of his contemporaries—in particular Plato, Aristophanes, and Xenophon—to reconstruct his life, trial, and death.

Accusation and Trial

Criminal proceedings in ancient Athens could be initiated by any citizen, and followed a well-defined path. They took place in several distinct stages, the first of which was accusation, and in the case of Socrates, his accuser was a poet, Meletus. The accused was summoned to appear before the legal magistrate for a preliminary hearing, at which the magistrate decided whether there was a case to answer. Having heard from both defendant and accuser, the magistrate found that there was indeed merit in the accusation against Socrates. At this point, formal charges were drawn up.

The document detailing the charges has now been lost, but is believed to have survived until at least the second century AD, and was recorded by Diogenes Laertius, in his *Lives and Opinions of Eminent Philosophers*, as reading: "This indictment and affidavit is sworn by Meletus of Pitthas against Socrates, the son of Sophroniscus of Alopece. Impiety—Socrates is guilty of refusing to recognize the gods recognized by the State; and of introducing other new divinities. He is also guilty of corrupting the youth. The penalty demanded is death."

The Death of Socrates (1787) by Jacques-Louis David. Socrates shows self-control in the face of death and demonstrates his commitment to his ideals, continuing to speak even while reaching for the poison. David would go on to become the court painter to Napoleon, according to some theories another famous victim of poisoning, possibly from arsenic in his wallpaper.

The size of the jury—selected by lottery from male volunteers aged over 30—reflected the significance of an Athenian trial, and the 500 jurors selected for the trial of Socrates indicated its importance. As was standard in Athens, the trial itself took place on a single day, and once the charges had been read, each side of the court made a three-hour speech presenting its case.

The prosecution spoke first, but no record remains of their argument. Of Socrates' response, two accounts survive—Plato's *Apology* and Xenophon's *Apology of Socrates to the Jury*. However, the speech Socrates made was anything but apologetic. Instead, he attacked his accusers and defiantly defended his own views. This aggressive and provocative stance stood in distinct contrast to normal defense speeches, which were typically a plea for mercy and attempted to play on the sympathies of the jury by introducing defendants' wives and children. Nor did this bold approach serve Socrates well—he was found guilty by 280 votes to 220.

Sentence and Death

Under Athenian law, each side of the court proposed a punishment, and the jury decided which to adopt. Socrates' accusers proposed execution, which at that time was accomplished by drinking the State Poison. Socrates himself chose not to opt for the standard counter-proposal—exile—and instead audaciously argued that he should be rewarded (he subsequently amended this to a meager fine). The jury voted for death by 360 votes to 140.

Socrates' behavior remains a mystery. By proposing a punishment that would inflame the jury, had he already accepted his fate? Most scholars see it as an act of martyrdom—a deliberate and provocative act that was the natural fulfillment of his ideals. His real motives cannot, of course, be known. However, if we accept that Socrates effectively chose to kill himself, this "execution" should perhaps be reclassified as suicide.

Plato recounts the course of Socrates' last minutes, and his somewhat peculiar last words, in testimony that would prove valuable to toxicological detectives seeking to solve the mystery of the State Poison.

After reproving his friends for indulging in loud lamentations, he continued to walk as he had been directed until he found his legs grow weary. Then he lay down upon his back and the person who had administered the poison went up to him and examined for some little time his feet and legs, and then squeezing his foot strongly asked whether he felt him. Socrates replied that he did not. He then did the same to his legs and proceeding upwards in this way, showed us that he was cold and stiff, and he afterwards approached him and said to us that when the effect of the poison reached his heart, Socrates would depart. And now the lower parts of his body were cold, when he uncovered himself and said, which were his last words, "Crito, we owe Asklepios a cock. Pay the debt and do not forget it."

An "Absolutely Irremediable" Substance

The State Poison is traditionally identified as hemlock, but this attribution elides one of the enduring mysteries of antiquity. Plato never refers directly to hemlock, describing the poison simply as *pharmakon*—"the drug"—while elsewhere it was described as a plant called *cicuta*, usually translated as "hemlock." But there was no contemporary description of this plant, and for many years

Poison hemlock, or *Conium maculatum*, is the most common of several species of hemlock noted for their toxicity. It contains several toxins, the most potent of which is coniine, a neurotoxin harmful to the nervous system. Similar in appearance to fennel, parsley, and wild carrot, the plant is native to Europe.

classicists were misled by a much later description of cicuta, by Nicander of Colophon, which described its toxic effects as violent convulsions.

The confusion stems from the existence of two species of hemlock: water hemlock (*Cicuta virosa*) and poison hemlock (*Conium maculatum*), which contain different toxins and produce differing effects (see right). Plato's account of the death of Socrates clearly describes a slow, relatively painless death—the hallmarks of a toxin acting on the peripheral nervous system, such as that found in poison hemlock. This identification was finally confirmed in a nineteenth-century report from Scottish toxicologist John Hughes Bennett, who attended a poor Edinburgh tailor who had eaten a "parsley sandwich" made for him by his children. In fact the parsley was poison hemlock, a close cousin, and the man suffered progressive paralysis similar to Socrates, eventually dying of respiratory paralysis.

But could there be more to the State Poison than just hemlock? Many ancient poisons were combinations of materials, and it seems likely that the Athenian *pharmakon* was no different. According to the Greek philosopher Theophrastus, the State Poison had been invented by the eminent herbalist Thrasyas of Mantineia in Arcadia: "By making use of the juices of cicuta, the poppy and such other things, he had discovered a substance which occasioned death easily and without pain, and so portable and minute that the weight of [about 60 grains, or roughly 4 g] was sufficient and absolutely irremediable."

In other words, the State Poison was most likely a mixture of poison hemlock extract and opium, the psychoactive effects of which might help to account for the last words of Socrates. Preparing this mixture was more of an art than a science, however, as illustrated by the account of a later execution, that of Phokion in 318 BC: "Having drunk all the cicuta, the quantity was found insufficient and the executioner refused to prepare more unless he was paid 12 drachmas."

HEMLOCK

Source:

Poison hemlock (*Conium maculatum*), also known as lesser hemlock, poison parsley, muskrat weed; water hemlock (*Cicuta virosa*) is a different species

Form:

Umbelliferous plant (resembles parsley and fennel, to which it is related)

Antidote:

Dimercaprol

Overview

Poison hemlock is essentially a weed, native to Europe and Asia but also common on both coasts of the U.S. Part of the same family as parsley, fennel, and carrots, it is easily mistaken for the former two. Normally around 3–6 ft tall, it has feathery bright green leaves and white flower heads. It can be distinguished from fennel by crushing the leaves and smelling them—they give off a disagreeable odor, said to resemble mouse urine. The whole plant is poisonous, although the concentration and distribution of the toxins changes as the plant ages. The two main toxins are alkaloids called coniine and coniceine. These are structurally similar to nicotine, and act on cholinergic receptors in the peripheral nervous system. Water hemlock is a related plant, found in marshes, ditches, and at the water's edge, which contains cicutoxin, a highly potent neurotoxin that acts on the central nervous system. Cicutoxin is most concentrated in the roots and a single bite can be fatal.

Symptoms

Initial symptoms of ingesting poison hemlock include gastritis and loss of co-ordination, which take effect within 30 minutes. The pulse becomes rapid and weak, vision dims, there is ascending paralysis (like that reported of Socrates), and gradual loss of movement. Consciousness is maintained throughout, until the victim suffocates from respiratory paralysis. There may be significant pain, contrary to the accounts of the ancient Greeks.

Despite these severe symptoms, deaths from hemlock poisoning are incredibly rare. It is a much greater problem for livestock, which may feed on it accidentally. It can also cause a type of fetal malformation known as "crooked calf disease" where pregnant cows feed on it.

Treatment

There is no specific antidote, so treatment is purely symptomatic. Thanks to its toxic properties, however, hemlock has a long history as a medicine itself. It was formerly believed to be effective in the treatment of scrofulous disorders, and Greek and Arabian physicians used it to treat tumors, swellings, and pains of the joints.

Famous Cases

Socrates
(469–399 BC)

THE DEATH OF THE DESERT FOX

Poison is often said to be the coward's weapon, which may explain why it has long appealed to fascists. An early example was that of Mussolini's blackshirt thugs, who were notorious for forcing political opponents to drink castor oil—a mild toxin, but administered in quantities that would cause violent purging of the bowels as well as vomiting. Sometimes they would mix it with petrol, in which case it could easily be fatal.

However, history also showed that fascists were liable not just to visit their poisonous predilections upon those outside their ranks; although at the high-water mark of Nazi success, no one would have believed that within a few short years the most celebrated German general of all would effectively be executed through forced suicide by poison pill.

A photo of Rommel taken on October 1, 1944, just two weeks before his forced suicide. The Field Marshal was convalescing at home in Germany after his car had been strafed.

As a young officer Erwin Rommel had won Germany's highest military honors in World War I, capturing thousands of Italians with a vastly inferior force during a daring attack in the Carpathians. Following Germany's resurgence he found himself the commander of a panzer division at the start of World War II and his rise continued as he proved an effective exponent of blitzkrieg tactics. In 1940 his division smashed through French defenses and wreaked havoc behind their lines. Then, at the head of the Afrika Korps, he overcame limited resources to inflict a series of stunning reversals on the British and gain himself further glory. He was Hitler's favorite general, the subject of relentless propaganda and hero-worship on the home front, and soon elevated to the rank of Field Marshal.

Valkyrie and D-Day

In 1943, after failing to convince Hitler to send much-needed reinforcements, Rommel was pulled out of Africa and put in command of the "Atlantic Wall," the reinforcement of the French coastline in anticipation of Allied invasion. Touring occupied Europe convinced Rommel that the war was unwinnable, and that Germany needed to sue for peace to avoid annihilation, and when it became clear that Hitler would never allow this, Rommel became disillusioned with the Führer. Other disgruntled officers who were fomenting Operation Valkyrie—the plot to assassinate Hitler—must have got wind of this and Rommel was approached. He refused to join the plot, but his limited involvement would come back to haunt him.

When D-Day came in June 1944, Rommel was on leave in Germany, but he raced back to the front and quickly assessed the position. Realizing that only a massive counterattack while the Allied beachhead was still fragile could head off disaster, he pleaded unsuccessfully with Hitler to commit tank divisions being held in reserve against a feared secondary invasion. Rommel could see that the war was lost, and on July 15 he infuriated the Nazi leader by telling him to negotiate an armistice. Two days later his staff car was strafed by two fighter planes with Royal Air Force markings, and he barely escaped with his life, suffering severe injuries. Interestingly, RAF records suggest that no planes were flying in the area at that time, suggesting to conspiracy theorists that Hitler was already planning to dispatch the dangerously popular but now "defeatist" general even before the events that followed.

On July 20 Hitler was attending a planning meeting in East Prussia, when a bomb in a suitcase exploded, killing four others but miraculously leaving him almost unscratched. Operation Valkyrie had failed and the reprisals were swift and brutal. Everyone connected to the plot was hunted down and killed, but Rommel posed a problem. Nazi propaganda had made him a popular hero; trying and executing him as a traitor would be a grievous blow to faltering national morale.

A Short Ride in the Car

On October 14, 15-year-old Manfred Rommel was given leave to visit his father, who was convalescing at the family home. The taint of suspicion hung over the Field Marshal, and senior members of his staff had already been executed for their purported roles in the Valkyrie plot. At midday Generals Burgdorf and Maisel arrived for a meeting with Rommel. He emerged a few minutes later and told his son gravely. "I have just had to tell your mother that I shall be dead in a quarter of an hour ... the house is surrounded and Hitler is charging me with high treason."

He explained that the generals had been sent to tell him that, "in view of my services in Africa, I am to have the chance of dying by poison. They have brought it with them. It's fatal in three seconds. If I accept, none of the usual steps will be taken against my family, that is, against you. They will also leave my staff alone."

Rommel put on his coat and got into the car with the generals and an SS driver. At 1.25 PM, on the road to the hospital in Ulm, the car pulled over and Burgdorf told Maisel and the driver to get out. When they got back in a few minutes later Rommel was slumped forward in his seat, his marshal's baton fallen from his hand. He had swallowed a cyanide pill. His death was publicly announced as the result of a brain seizure and he was given a full state funeral, at which the largest wreath, of course, came from Hitler.

GASSING AND LETHAL INJECTIONS

When Thrasyas of Mantineia first created the State Poison of Athens (see pp. 96–100) he was initiating a long search for more "humane" ways to execute people. In the modern era, most states that have resolved to kill someone in the name of justice are ever more intent upon avoiding "cruel and unusual" methods of execution; indeed in the U.S. these are specifically legislated against.

Modern efforts to find a humane means of execution can be traced back to the 1840s, with Robert Christison's daring experiments with the Calabar Bean. Also known as the Ordeal or Killer Bean of Calabar, this contains physostigmine, a potent neurotoxin (see pp. 94–5), discovered in part thanks to Christison's decision to test its toxicity on himself. Swallowing steadily larger doses of bean, he reported that although he suffered various dangerous symptoms he at no time experienced any pain. This led to suggestions that the bean might make for a more humane mode of execution than hanging.

In 1888 a similar train of thought led a New York doctor, J. Mount Bleyer, to suggest in an article in the *Medico–Legal Journal* that an intravenous injection of six grains of morphine (nearly 400 mg, about two and a half times the lethal dose for a normal adult who has never used opiates before, but significantly less than many addicts can tolerate) would be a more humane option for execution while avoiding the public spectacle of a hanging, which was felt to imbue the prisoner with heroic status. New York State decided to introduce the electric chair instead, with horrific consequences. The device was introduced partly as a publicity stunt by Thomas Edison, who was attempting to show that a rival's electricity system was dangerous. He was wrong, with the result that the unfortunate prisoner, William Kemmler, had to be shocked repeatedly, with his blood boiling, veins bursting, and skin catching fire, in what one contemporary report decried as "an awful spectacle."

The Chamber of Death

The next attempt to use poison as a humane method of execution came with the introduction of the gas chamber in the U.S. in the 1920s. The first man to be killed in this way was Gee Jon, a Chinese-American gangster convicted of murder in a Tong turf war in Nevada. Initially the state tried to pump cyanide gas into his cell while he slept, but this ham-fisted attempt foundered when the gas leaked out of the unsealed cell and dissipated, so an airtight chamber was constructed instead.

Since then most American gas chamber executions have followed a similar procedure, in which the condemned is strapped to a chair or bed inside an airtight chamber with a viewing window. A long stethoscope leads into the chamber and is affixed to the prisoner so that a doctor can declare him or her dead. Cyanide salts are used to generate hydrogen cyanide gas, either by dropping pellets of sodium cyanide into a pail of sulphuric acid, or by running acid onto pellets of potassium cyanide. The result is the same: a cloud of gas is released, which produces a violent reaction in the prisoner.

For a supposedly humane alternative, death is remarkably unpleasant. Clifton Duffy, former warden of San Quentin penitentiary in California, describes the process: "At first there is evidence of extreme horror, pain, and strangling. The eyes pop. The skin turns purple and the victim begins to drool." The cyanide disrupts the ATP pathways in the mitochondria, effectively cutting off energy production in cells (see p. 20). Experts suggest that the sensation is similar to having a massive heart attack, and death results as the brain runs out of oxygen. The process should take just a few minutes, but in some notorious executions prisoners have taken up to eleven minutes to die.

After the prisoner is pronounced dead, the prison staff face the difficult task of decontaminating the chamber and retrieving the body. An exhaust fan evacuates the chamber and the cyanide gas is treated with ammonia to neutralize it—although ammonia itself is toxic. The corpse is also sprayed with ammonia, and after half an hour has elapsed orderlies in protective clothing enter the chamber. They are advised to ruffle the corpse's hair to release any trapped gas.

Not only is the process expensive and dangerous, but the death throes of the condemned have convinced many people—including a federal judge in California—that execution by gas chamber does in fact constitute a "cruel and unusual punishment." Perhaps for this reason, although several states in the U.S. still have working gas chambers, they are not presently used, and the last person to be killed in this fashion was Walter LaGrand in Arizona in 1999.

Lethal Injection

Lethal injection is now the most popular form of execution, both in the U.S. and elsewhere. In 2007, for instance, all but one of the 42 executions in the U.S. were carried out by lethal injection, and it has also been adopted by the Philippines, Guatemala, and Thailand.

This grim room was the Nevada state gas chamber in Carson City, photographed in 1926. Nevada was the first state to kill a condemned man with gas, with the 1924 execution of Gee Jon.

The modern protocol for lethal injections was first introduced in Oklahoma in 1977, where it had been drawn up by the state's Chief Medical Examiner, Jay Chapman, but was not actually used until 1982, when Charles Brooks Jr. was executed by the state of Texas.

The procedure, which has largely been followed ever since, involves strapping the condemned to a gurney and using a catheter to put a line into a vein in each arm. These are flushed with anti-clotting solution and saline—which is flushed through between each drug, to prevent the drugs reacting and precipitating out of solution. The first drug is a short-acting barbiturate, sodium thiopental, intended to knock the victim out immediately and suppress central nervous system function to a lethal extent. Then a muscle relaxant, pancuronium bromide, paralyzes the diaphragm to cause suffocation. Lastly a large dose of potassium chloride floods the cardiovascular system with potassium and stops the heart. The whole process is supposed to take three to five minutes. Sometimes the drugs are administered via a machine, which has two buttons, one of which operates a dummy system and the other the real one—in this way the two executioners do not know who is truly responsible.

Brooks's execution seemed to go off smoothly, and he was observed simply to clench his fist, take a deep breath, and pass out. But in the years since a range of issues has suggested that lethal injection is not the humane alternative it appears. For instance, doctors cannot be directly involved in the execution for ethical reasons, so I.V. lines must be fitted by orderlies. This can be difficult at the best of times, but especially on the many condemned prisoners who are intravenous drug abusers, and on whom it is difficult to find a vein. In many executions this means that surgical incisions are made to insert the line in the groin; in others it has led to the undignified spectacle of the prisoner helping the orderlies find a vein and insert the I.V.

Even worse, recent research by a group at the University of Miami suggests that there is a real possibility that the anesthesia induced by the sodium thiopental is insufficient, and that in fact the prisoner is conscious, but paralyzed and unable to signal. There is also evidence that the potassium dose may be insufficient to stop the heart. Trapped in paralysis, the prisoner suffocates while fully conscious, which calls the "humane" rationale into question.

POISON IN MASS EXECUTION

Given the capacity of toxic gas to poison and kill large numbers of people without creating too much blood, gore, or collateral physical damage, perhaps inevitably it has appealed to genocidal mass murderers. The most notorious examples of this are the crimes of the Nazis and their infamous gas chambers, but in a controversial 2005 book, *Le Crime de Napoléon*, French historian Claude Ribbe claims that the Little Corsican was a criminal to match Hitler—who, perhaps not coincidentally, was a huge fan of the emperor and paid homage at his tomb after the conquest of Paris.

After the Haitian slave uprising of the late eighteenth century, Napoleon sent his brother-in-law Charles Leclerc to reinstate French control and, says Ribbe, perpetrate a hideous act of genocide in order to clear the way for the importation of a fresh crop of more pliant, docile slaves. General Leclerc was allegedly given orders to kill as many black Haitians as possible, and pursued his remit with ghastly vigor. In particular, says Ribbe, on the direct orders of Napoleon, sulfur was extracted from deposits on the flanks of Haitian volcanoes, and then burned to produce the poisonous gas, sulfur dioxide. This was employed on prison ships with sealed holds, known as *étouffiers*—"chokers." "Victims of both sexes were piled up, one against the other," wrote a contemporary historian who had sailed with the expedition; the poisonous sulfur gas was then pumped into the holds to suffocate them en masse. Up to 100,000 people were murdered in the course of Leclerc's reign of terror.

Nazi Gas Vans

A more recent parallel can be found in the history of the Second World War. As the German Army moved east, through Poland and later the Soviet Union, special units, or *Einsatzgruppen*, followed in their wake with orders to exterminate political undesirables and Jews. Most of their victims were shot, but this was laborious, messy, and bad for morale; as SS-Obersturmbannführer Walter Rauff later complained, "At the time the most important consideration for me was the psychological stress felt by the men involved in the shootings." He went on to explain that "This problem was overcome by the use of gas vans."

The idea for gas vans stemmed from the previous use of poison gas as part of the euthanasia program. After messy experiments with explosives, it was found that running the exhaust fumes from two cars into a sealed ward of the mental asylum in Mogilev, in the Ukraine, killed the inmates quickly. Rauff oversaw the realization and escalation of this concept to produce modified trucks with sealed cabins, into which exhaust fumes rich in carbon monoxide were piped. Up to 150 people at a time could be packed into the back of the truck and gassed, and eventually around 30 gas vans were made and deployed.

Zyklon B

More infamous still than the Nazis' use of gas vans was the deployment of Zyklon or Cyclon B. An insecticide first made in Germany in the 1920s, the "B" stands for *Blausäure*, German for prussic acid, or hydrocyanic acid (hydrogen cyanide in solution). The cyanide, together with a stabilizer and a warning odorant—a strong-smelling substance to serve as a warning that the material was toxic—were impregnated into absorbent pellets, usually of silica gel. These were stored in airtight containers; then, when they were dispensed, they would release hydrogen cyanide gas. In the 1930s Zyklon B was used in the U.S. to disinfect and delouse immigrants' clothes, and in Nazi concentration camps it was also initially used to prevent the spread of typhus.

The relative success of the Einsatzgruppen gas vans led the high-ranking Nazis responsible for the Final Solution to look at using gas to accomplish mass exterminations. Carbon monoxide from engine exhausts was used in some camps but Zyklon B was much more potent and was the agent used in the worst death camps at Auschwitz-Birkenau and Mjdanek. After initial tests on 250 gypsy children in early 1940, the first trial at Auschwitz was carried out in September 1941. Some 600 Soviet prisoners of war and 250 sick Polish prisoners were crammed into a bunker, and pellets of Zyklon B were dropped through a vent.

Zyklon B was a tradename for a product originally developed for pest control. Originally the pellets, or "crystals," were impregnated with a warning odorant, but when production switched to supplying the gas chambers the odorant was removed. Under the tradename Uragan D-2 it is still manufactured in the Czech Republic, as a "disinfecting, disinfesting fumigation agent."

The trial was considered a success and two bunkers were constructed to hold 2,000 people between them.

Using pellets of Zyklon B up to 8,000 people a day could be gassed at Auschwitz-Birkenau alone. It took about 20 minutes for everyone in the chamber to die, and although those close to the vents perished quickly, for others there was unimaginable horror and pain. SS doctor Joann Kremer later testified that, "Shouting and screaming of the victims could be heard through the opening and it was clear that they fought for their lives."

Although the dark chapter of mass gassings in Nazi death camps has closed, it has not marked the end of the gas chamber. Apart from their use in judicial executions, chilling evidence has recently emerged that scientists at North Korea's largest concentration camp, Camp 22, have been gassing groups of people, including whole families, in ghastly experiments. In 2004 the ex-chief of the camp told the BBC, "I witnessed a whole family being tested on suffocating gas and dying in the gas chamber." He described a "glass chamber" that was sealed airtight, enabling scientists to view the experiments from above. Further evidence suggests that chemical weapons are being tested in these gas chambers.

CHAPTER FIVE

POISON

AS

ASSASSIN

"The coward's weapon, poison."

John Fletcher (1579–1625)

THE USE OF POISON AS AN ASSASSIN'S WEAPON OF CHOICE HAS A RICH AND EVOC-ATIVE HISTORY. AND THE POLITICAL OR MILITARY MOTIVATIONS THAT LIE BEHIND EACH ASSASSINATION ONLY SERVE TO ADD TO THE INTRIGUE AND MYSTERY THAT ENSHROUDS THESE SHADOWY KILLINGS.

The reasons that poison was once the perfect tool for assassination are three-fold. First, its delayed but irremediable effects allow the assassin to make good his or her escape, such as in the modern poisoning of Alexander Litvinenko (see pp. 136–9), whoever administered the poison was long gone by the time it had taken effect, and although there are suspects there is little chance of ever being certain who was responsible.

Second, until relatively recently most poisons were difficult to detect and therefore hard to guard against, and even harder to identify after the event. For instance, the poison employed by the Borgias (see pp. 78–9) was said to have a slightly sweet taste, easily masked by highly spiced food. Moreover, many poisons cause symptoms similar to naturally occurring illnesses—it is suspected, for instance, that Josef Stalin was poisoned, but even advocates of the theory have to admit that the symptoms he displayed were consistent with the official cause of death, cerebral hemorrhage.

Finally, poison allows for ingenious methods of administration that can pierce even the most stringent safeguards, and history records actual or proposed assassinations using everything from poisoned books and gloves to cigars and umbrellas.

CLASSICAL ASSASSINATIONS

History tends to record the lives, and particularly the deaths, of the great and glorious, who also comprise the natural constituency of the assassin. As a result, much of the early history of the use of poison is, more precisely, the history of poison as an assassin's weapon.

Poison was especially important for clearing the path to succession, partly because it enabled usurpers to topple rulers without appearing to have committed an obvious crime, but also because it was the often the only available tool for women in politics. One legendary example from ancient times concerns the fourth-century BCE Persian queen Parysatis. According to Plutarch and Ctesias, Parysatis assassinated her daughter-in-law Statira by smearing with venom one side of a carving knife, which she used to divide the game bird that had been served for dinner. She served the poisoned half to Statira and ate her half with impunity.

The Deadly Empresses of Rome

Thanks to Robert Graves's novel *I, Claudius*, the poisonous habits of the two first ladies of imperial Rome, Livia Augusta and Agrippina the Younger, have entered the popular consciousness. However, Graves drew on the work of Roman historians such as Tacitus and Cassius Dio, who were either repeating scurrilous rumors or blackening the women's names for reasons of their own. Indeed it is often the case that many of the tales of perfidious poisoners throughout history, from Livia to Catherine de Medici, may owe more to propaganda than truth. The fiction, however, is far too entertaining to ignore.

Livia was the wife of Augustus, the first emperor of Rome, and is considered by most historians today to have been a devoted wife and a capable and indomitable woman who worked alongside her husband to accomplish his imperial agenda. In Graves's version of history, however, she was ruthless and cunning, using assassination to ensure the succession would pass to her son from a previous marriage, Tiberius. One by one the possible rivals to his inheritance perished until finally only Augustus himself stood between Tiberius and the imperial throne—and by extension between Livia and power, for she expected to exert considerable influence on her son.

Augustus died in AD 14, and both Tacitus and Cassius Dio repeat rumors that Livia killed him by painting figs with poison while they were still on the tree, and then encouraging him to pick and eat those ones, while she picked safe ones close by to allay any suspicions he might have. Her favored poison is sometimes said to have been belladonna (see p. 52).

Locusta's School of Poisoners

Even more notorious was the empress Agrippina, wife of Claudius and mother of Nero. Beautiful and deadly, she is said to have murdered her first husband in order to be free to marry Claudius, and then to have rescued from prison a Gallic woman named Locusta, a convicted poisoner. Together with Nero, she supposedly set Locusta up as a sort of state poisoner, supplying her with slaves upon whom to experiment.

Claudius was known to be particularly fond of mushrooms, and the death cap is often implicated in his death. But Claudius's symptoms—diarrhea, salivation, low blood pressure, wheezing, vomiting, and abdominal pain—more closely match those caused by the fly agaric, which though less toxic, can cause death more quickly if given in a high enough dose.

Of course, it is possible that Claudius, who suffered poor health, died of natural causes, but there is no question that Agrippina had both the motive and opportunity, having coincidentally dispatched Claudius's loyal freedman Narcissus to the beach, supposedly to recuperate from a case of gout.

After Claudius's death in AD 54 Nero acceded to the throne, but Claudius's son by his previous marriage, Britannicus, still posed a threat to his position. Locusta, therefore, supplied a poison that was administered by the cunning ruse of mixing it with cold water, in the knowledge that Britannicus would call for some to add to some soup that was too hot. Nero, who was present, remained unmoved when Britannicus started convulsing, merely remarking that he too had often had such fits in his youth. The feast continued but Britannicus did not.

Inevitably, within a few years Nero fell out with his mother and devised ingenious ways to dispatch her. According to one story he attempted to drown her by sending her to sea in a boat weighted with a heavy lead deck. The deck collapsed but Agrippina fortuitously survived, and when the crew scuttled the ship she got clear and swam back to shore to the applause of

onlookers. Another account has Nero trying to poison her on three separate occasions, only for her to outfox him with the antidote each time. Eventually he resorted to having her stabbed and passing it off as suicide. Locusta, meanwhile, fell foul of the law again in AD 55, but was saved by Nero from execution, although her days were numbered as she was eventually put to death by Galba in AD 69.

The Italian Vice

In the centuries that followed a host of emperors were suspected of being either poisoners or poisoned—Domitian, for example, of poisoning his wife to cause an abortion, and Commodus of being poisoned by his wife Marcia (although he looked set to survive, so was finished off by smothering).

Perhaps there was something about assassination by poison that appealed to the Italian psyche, because it again became prominent in the Middle Ages, in Venice with the Council of Ten (see p. 78) and in Rome under the Borgias (see pp. 78–9). Around the same time, an Italian princess, Catherine de Medici, was said to have brought the dark art of poisoning to France, where she was accused of wielding it against political rivals.

Catherine's first victim was widely suspected to be her husband's older brother, François, who stood between her and the French throne. François fell ill after asking his secretary, Sébastien Montecuccoli, for a cup of water to cool down after a game of tennis. When the young dauphin died a few days later, Montecuccoli—an Italian brought over by Catherine—was suspected of having poisoned him, and supposedly confessed under torture after a book on poisons was found in his quarters. It seems equally likely, however, that the dauphin died of tuberculosis, for his health was known to have been ruined by a youth spent locked in a Spanish prison. Despite retracting his confession, Montecuccoli was executed in Lyon by being torn apart by four horses.

Catherine de Medici (1519–89), the Florentine princess who became Queen of France and was accused of poisoning her political rivals, painted by the Italian artist Santi di Tito in 1585–6.

MURDER IN THE TOWER

Court intrigue is a delicate game, in which concealed assassination can be the trump card or the joker. So it proved in the ugly and tragic tale of Sir Thomas Overbury, poet and counselor to the king's favorite at the court of James I, in early seventeenth-century England.

Renowned for his close friendships—which have led many historians to speculate about his sexuality—James I showered titles on his favorites, foremost among them the handsome and ambitious Robert Carr. Carr in turn had an intimate friend in Thomas Overbury, a poet and courtier, and indeed Overbury and the king may also have had relations. As Carr ascended the ranks of nobility, so Overbury rode on his coat-tails; but while Carr had the ear of the king, he relied on the more capable Overbury for the counsel he gave to James.

In the end, it was a woman who came between the two men. Carr had been carrying on an affair with the beautiful Frances Howard, scion of one of the most powerful families in the kingdom. As a young teenager she had been married off to the Earl of Essex, but had taken care to ensure that the relationship was never consummated, intending to take advantage of a law that allowed for annulment after three years of unconsummated marriage. To this end she employed a dressmaker, Ann Turner, who in turn was friends with a notorious astrologer and magician, Simon Forman—and together they supplied Frances with spells and magic dolls to ward off Essex and charm Carr.

By 1613 Frances was ready to annul her marriage, freeing her to marry Carr. At first Overbury had drafted love letters and poems for Carr, but when he learned that the relationship might be more than a casual affair he began to fear that he would lose his influence and power if his protector were to be drawn into the Howard circle. Accordingly he began to vilify Frances, warning Carr that, "if you do marry that base woman, you will utterly ruin your honor and yourself. You shall never do it with my advice or consent; and, if you do, you had best look to stand fast."

Carr was furious but also anxious. Overbury guarded many embarrassing secrets, secrets that could ruin him. So Carr and Frances resolved to remove his erstwhile friend from the scene, setting in motion an elaborate scheme. In 1613 Carr secretly arranged for Overbury to be offered undesirable ambassadorial positions overseas, and then encouraged him to turn them down. The king, offended, ordered him to be locked in the Tower of London.

Letters to the Tower

Carr and Frances now had Overbury in their grasp, because Carr's man Sir Gervase Elwes was shortly to take over as Lieutenant of the Tower, where he would be able to control access to Overbury and provide opportunities to strike.

With Mrs. Turner's help, Frances obtained poisons from an apothecary and experimented with them on a series of unfortunate cats. Realgar, or arsenic sulfide, proved highly effective, and was duly slipped into Overbury's broth on May 9, just a few days after Elwes took over at the Tower. He suffered violent diarrhea and vomiting but survived this and a second, larger dose. Overbury even hoped that his illness would encourage the king to have mercy, expressing these hopes in letters to Carr, who was duplicitously maintaining a friendly correspondence.

Overbury had pinned his hopes of release on a meeting of the Privy Council on July 6. He wrote to Carr that he planned to take an emetic to make himself appear even more ill, unwittingly offering his enemies another chance to make an attempt on his life. Frances and Mrs. Turner obtained some white arsenic and arranged for it to be mixed with the emetic powder, which Overbury took on July 1. He was horribly ill for four days, with constant vomiting and purging of the bowels, raging fever, and a constant thirst. "In truth I never liked myself worse," he wrote to Carr, "for I can endure no clothes on, and do nothing but drink," although this latter claim was not entirely accurate, for it was reported that he also voided his bowels over 50 times.

The Privy Council did not see fit to release him, but Overbury lived on. Frances resolved to try corrosive sublimate—a mercury poison—mixing it into some tarts and jellies sent to the Tower on July 19. In a note to Elwes,

Frances warned him, "The tarts or jelly taste you not of, but the wine you may drink, for in it is no letters, I know"—"letters" being her somewhat unsubtle code for poison.

The poisoned food was duly fed to Overbury who became even sicker than before. His suspicions began to mount that Carr was "juggling" him, and he started to write conciliatory letters to the Howard family, begging for help. In late August, however, the Lieutenant of the Tower cut off all correspondence and moved him to a smaller cell. Now desperate, Overbury penned a letter to Carr threatening to reveal sordid details that would "make you the most odious man alive." It was time to finish him off, and William Reeves, the young assistant to an apothecary who was treating the unfortunate prisoner, was paid to administer an enema of corrosive sublimate.

On September 13, 1613, Reeves administered the enema, and the next morning poor Overbury breathed his last. His body was in a piteous state, wizened, stinking, and covered with ulcers, sores, and blisters. Soon afterwards the king convened an Annulment Commission, which ruled that Frances was free to marry Carr, by now the Earl of Somerset. And when the two were married—in a lavish ceremony in December—it seemed their plot had succeeded.

A Guilty Conscience

Less than two years later, however, their conspiracy began to unravel. In June 1615 Reeves, now living in Holland, was struck down ill and, fearing for both his life and his immortal soul, he made a confession that was relayed to the English secretary of state Sir Ralph Winwood who, in turn, prompted the king to commission an investigation. Within months the lesser players in the conspiracy had been brought to book—Elwes, Mrs. Turner, and a number of others were hanged.

Carr and Frances were tried in May 1616 and sent to the Tower, but the king spared them execution, and eventually pardoned and released them. Young Reeves survived his brush with death, returned to England, and escaped prosecution altogether. Poor Overbury at least enjoyed posthumous success with a best-selling poem, *The Wife*.

RASPUTIN, THE UNKILLABLE MAN

An illiterate Siberian peasant, Grigory Rasputin spent time in a monastery and was linked to the controversial Khlysty sect, who practiced energetic self-flagellation and were rumored to believe that orgiastic depravity offered a shortcut to heaven. After years of wandering, he pitched up as a *starets*—a mystic or faith healer—in St. Petersburg, where he gained a reputation for working wonders. He soon came to the attention of Tsarina Aleksandra, who was desperately searching for a way to treat her hemophiliac son Aleksei. Where all others had failed, Rasputin somehow succeeded.

Rasputin, the Russian monk who rose to power through his reputed mystic powers and "unnatural" influence over Aleksandra, the Russian empress.

Rasputin became the tsarina's counsellor and confidant, wielding great power and abusing it in order to indulge his capacious lust for sex and drink. The aristocracy loathed and feared him. World War I was going disastrously for the Russians, and with the tsar away at the front Rasputin's influence was greater than ever. Many believed he was the tsarina's lover, and was inciting her to make a separate peace with the Germans. It is more likely that, appalled at the vast casualties and the miserable lot of the Russian soldier, Rasputin simply doubted the wisdom of continuing a disastrous war.

The Prince's Plot

Opinion among Russia's elite was hardening against Rasputin when outspoken politician Vladimir Purishkevich gave a rousing speech against him in the Russian parliament in November 1916. Purishkevich was then approached by Prince Felix Yusupov, husband of the tsar's niece, about joining in a plot to do away with the Mad Monk. Together with Grand Duke Dmitry Pavlovich, Dr. Lazovert, a physician, and others, Yusupov planned to lure Rasputin to his house, murder him, and dump the body through a hole in the ice of the frozen Malaya Nevka River, where it would not be recovered until the spring thaw.

The specifics of the murder are unclear, since the conspirators' accounts differ, but it seems that something along the following lines took place:

Under the guise of needing his healing powers, Yusupov effected an introduction to Rasputin. Once he had befriended him, he lured him to his house on the evening of December 16, apparently on the pretext that Yusupov's beautiful wife Irina wanted to meet and possibly bestow her favors upon him. Yusupov and the doctor picked Rasputin up in their car and invited him to take tea in the dining room. "While Rasputin was drinking tea," explained Yusupov in his 1926 memoir, "I was to administer a solution of potassium of cyanide." Dr. Lazovert claims that it was he who administered the poison, donning rubber gloves to crush some crystals into a chocolate cake and a glass of wine.

Rasputin greedily consumed the food and wine but appeared unaffected—one theory to account for this is that sugar reacts with cyanide to form non-toxic compounds that can be excreted, so that by adding the cyanide to cake and sweet wine the conspirators were actually premixing the poison with its antidote. To Yusupov's dismay, Rasputin called for his host to "Play something cheerful. I like to hear you sing."

Instead the prince went upstairs to get a revolver. "'Where shall I shoot him,' I thought, 'through the temple or through the heart?'" he later wrote, but according to most accounts he actually shot Rasputin in the back. The plotters watched the monk apparently give up his last breath, but when Yusupov came back to check on him later he was still alive, "bellowing and snorting like a wounded animal." They shot him three more times, before Yusupov went into a frenzy and tried to beat in his head with a dumbbell. Finally they wrapped him in a sheet and dumped him into an icy river as planned. When the body was recovered several days later it appeared that, incredibly, Rasputin had still been alive at this point and managed to free his arms before freezing and drowning.

The British Connection

This amazing tale, which served to emphasize the inhuman and devilish nature of the assassinated man, soon passed into popular legend, but the evidence does not entirely support it. For example, the autopsy failed to find any trace of poison, and although it did give the cause of death as hypothermia from the river, it also noted a gunshot wound in the center of Rasputin's forehead, the hallmark of a professional hit. What's more, the bullet in question was almost certainly a type fired only by the service revolvers of British officers.

Some accounts of the assassination do indeed record the presence of at least one Briton, Oswald Rayner, a friend of the prince, but also an officer in the British Secret Service Bureau. Other evidence has since come to light that strongly suggests that Rayner fired the fatal shot, as part of a British plan to ensure that Rasputin did not persuade the Russian royals to make peace with the Germans, freeing up the German army to throw its full weight against the Western Front. The tale of Rasputin's superhuman resistance to massive doses of cyanide was probably part of a cover story intended to conceal this daring state-sponsored assassination.

CYANIDE

Source:
Apple seeds, apricot pits, almonds, cassava root; also fires and cigarette smoke

Form:
White crystalline powder in salt form; colorless volatile liquid as hydrogen cyanide

Antidotes:
Nitrites, hydroxocobalamin, 4-DMAP, kelocyanor (cobalt salt)

Overview
Cyanide is dangerous because its ion binds very strongly to several metals that the body uses as an important part of many enzymes, and in particular with the iron atom that sits at the core of an enzyme called cytochrome c oxidase (CCO), found in mitochondria. CCO is the final link in a chain of enzymes that transfer electrons—its job is to transfer electrons to oxygen molecules, a vital step that drives the process of cellular respiration, wherein oxygen is burned to release energy and drive all the processes of the cell. When the cyanide ion gets into a cell, it quickly binds to the iron atom in CCO, preventing it from functioning and stopping the cell from using oxygen. It effectively suffocates the cell, or, to use the technical term, causes histotoxic anoxia. Cyanide is also toxic in other ways, unleashing cascades of oxidative damage (see p. 20), but hypoxia is the main effect.

Symptoms
A massive dose of cyanide, such as that provided by suicide pills, kills so rapidly that other symptoms simply do not have time to manifest. Smaller but nonetheless acute doses can cause brief stimulation of the CNS, followed by convulsions, low blood pressure, slow heart rate, loss of consciousness, lung damage, and respiratory failure, followed by coma and death. Sub-lethal doses can cause rapid and difficult breathing, confusion, headaches, giddiness, vomiting, and palpitations.

Treatment
Different countries use different antidotes. Cobalt salts such as kelocyanor chelate the cyanide ion to produce a harmless complex that can be filtered by the kidneys (see pp. 17–18), but the salts themselves can be toxic.

FAMOUS CASES

Grigory Rasputin
(1869–1916)

Erwin Rommel
(1891–1944)

Adolf Hitler
(1889–1945)

Alan Turing
(1912–54)

Jonestown Massacre
(1978)

THE CHAMBER

Ever since the early days of what became the KGB and is now the FSB, the Russian secret service pursued an aggressive policy of elimination of opponents wherever they were. A hallmark of these operations was plausible deniability, and to this end the assassinations were often carried out with poisons that were carefully developed to be extremely difficult to identify, detect, and trace. To produce such highly specialized weapons, the Russian secret services turned to a sinister top-secret research institute, variously known as *Kamera*—Russian for "the Chamber"—Laboratory No. 1, Laboratory No. 12, the Central Investigation Institute for Special Technology, "Russia's poison factory," and "the laboratory of death."

Mairanovsky's Experiments

Originally set up in the 1920s, Kamera came into its own in 1939 with the appointment of biochemist Grigory Mairanovsky as its new director. Starting with mustard gas (see pp. 202–4), he worked to develop ever more deadly and undetectable toxic agents, and has been accused by several sources of experimenting on humans, specifically prisoners from the gulags. When the former head of Stalin's secret intelligence empire, Lavrentiy Beria, was put on trial for his life in the 1950s, he confirmed that this vile practice had taken place, admitting: "I gave orders to Mairanovsky to conduct experiments on people sentenced to the highest measure of punishment, but it was not my idea."

Mairanovsky was eventually arrested and tried in one of the Soviet state's purges, and was imprisoned for a decade, but Kamera lived on, although it passed through various incarnations. Since the breakdown of the USSR there have been fears that, like other secret services, it has hired itself out to business and mafia organizations, and that even Russian presidents—Vladimir Putin, a former head of the FSB among them—do not have full knowledge of or control over its activities.

Special Equipment

Kamera's trademark has been to treat existing toxins in novel ways to make them harder to identify, trace, and treat. The recent attempted assassination of Victor Yushchenko and the successful murder of Alexander Litvinenko (see pp. 136–9), both bear the hallmarks of an operation using "special equipment"—as Kamera-supplied poisons were euphemistically known—which proved extremely difficult to identify and, even when they were pinned down, baffled experts because of their strange characteristics.

An earlier example of a classic Kamera-supplied operation was the 1957 killing of anti-Soviet émigré writer Lev Rebet, who was sprayed with cyanide mist from a spray-gun concealed in a rolled-up newspaper. For four years it was thought that Rebet had died from a heart attack, until the assassin involved defected to the West and revealed his part in the plot.

Two years before this, another Russian émigré, Georgy Okolovich, had narrowly escaped assassination by means of a poisoned bullet to be fired from a miniature pistol concealed within a cigarette packet. Then Nikolay Khokhlov—the man who was to carry out this assassination, but defected instead—was himself the subject of an attempted assassination in 1955, when poison was slipped into his coffee at a public reception. Tests revealed traces of thallium, a toxic metal later much favored by assassins working for Saddam Hussein, but the appropriate treatments did not seem to work. Eventually doctors worked out that Khokhlov had been given thallium treated with radioactivity, which changed its properties and action, so that it would be untraceable. Khokhlov survived, but over the years a great many other victims have not.

Kamera also served as a real-life counterpart to the fictional "Q" from James Bond, coming up with fantastical and ingenious methods to deliver its deadly toxins. The spray-gun and cigarette-packet pistol above are just two examples; perhaps the most famous of these imaginative weapons was the poison pellet-firing umbrella supplied to the Bulgarian secret service for use in the assassination of Georgi Markov.

THE UMBRELLA ASSASSIN

One of the Cold War's most enduring mysteries is the assassination of Bulgarian dissident Georgi Markov by an umbrella-wielding assassin in London in 1978. Markov is believed to have been murdered with one of the deadliest poisons in nature; one that is easily synthesized from readily available natural sources, is highly toxic even in minute quantities, cannot be detected or guarded against, and for which there is no antidote. Thirty years on, a crusading reporter claims to have finally identified Markov's assassin, bringing to a climax a lurid tale of secret Soviet biological warfare research, lethal gadgetry straight out of a Bond movie, and a personal tragedy that resonates today more than ever.

The Truth That Killed

In the 1960s Georgi Markov was a bestselling Bulgarian author and successful playwright whose work met with official approval and who mixed with the country's cultural and political elite, including Communist Party leaders. He was privy to the carefully guarded details of their private lives and personal secrets. But by the late '60s he was disillusioned with what he called the "moral degradation" of Bulgarian socialist society, and in particular with the corrosive interference in the cultural life of the country by its capricious and autocratic leader Todor Zhivkov. In the face of growing official displeasure over his increasingly critical plays, Markov fled to the West, moving first to Italy to stay with his brother and later to London to start a new life as a journalist, writer, and cultural commentator. He was branded a traitor by the Bulgarian state and tried and sentenced in absentia.

In 1975 he began broadcasting on the CIA-sponsored Radio Free Europe, and for the next three years his weekly shows about culture and politics in Bulgaria gained a huge audience throughout his native country—the scripts were later collected and published as a book called *The Truth That Killed*. But in telling the truth about the nation's corrupt political elite, its venality and hypocrisy, and its perversion of culture and even language, Markov was putting his life in real danger. After the Bulgarian authorities cruelly refused him permission to visit his dying father in 1977, Markov commenced a series of personal attacks on Zhivkov. Anonymous death threats failed to silence him, and the Bulgarian secret police are believed to have called on their Soviet big brothers to help get rid of this turbulent journalist. Two botched assassination attempts followed, but on September 7, 1978—President Zhivkov's sixty-seventh birthday—Markov was the target of a third, and this time successful attempt; one of the most ingenious of the entire Cold War.

Murder on Waterloo Bridge

The Soviet regimes of the Cold War saw nothing wrong with extrajudicial killing, in other words assassination, of those they considered enemies of Communism. And the KGB was detailed to research the most effective ways to accomplish such killings, without leaving traces or evidence to connect them to the crime. Poison was a popular method, and Soviet research pointed in particular to ricin, an extremely potent toxin that was undetectable, untreatable, and untraceable. To be effective, however, it needed to be inhaled, ingested, or injected, and to this end one of the most unlikely weapons of the Cold War was invented.

That fateful September morning, just two weeks after an anonymous phone call had warned Georgi Markov that he would die of "natural causes" thanks to a potent, "invisible" poison, the Bulgarian was waiting for a bus at a stop on London's Waterloo Bridge in the heart of the capital. Feeling a sudden sharp stinging sensation he whirled round and saw a man with his back to him, bending over to retrieve a dropped umbrella. "I'm sorry," muttered the man in a foreign accent, before hailing a taxi cab that drove him away.

Markov tried to shrug off the incident but his leg hurt and there was blood on his jeans and a swelling like a bite-mark on his thigh. By the evening he had developed a high fever, and the next day he was admitted to hospital, struggling to speak. The doctors suspected septicemia, or blood poisoning, but Markov did not respond to treatment and his symptoms became progressively

The castor-oil plant, *Ricinus communis*, which contains the potent toxin ricin. Despite its deadly content the plant also has a long history of medicinal use. The seed is rich in oil, which, since ricin is water-soluble, is toxin-free. It can be used in cooking, but has also been used a laxative for at least 2,000 years. Its purgative effects mean that castor oil has even been used to treat victims of poisoning. Castor seeds are used in traditional Tibetan medicine and elsewhere to treat digestive disorders including parasitic worms, and also for skin problems and headaches. Castor oil is even said to have anti-dandruff properties.

worse. His blood pressure dropped, his kidneys began to fail, and he started vomiting blood. Fluid collected in his lungs, making it hard for him to breathe, and on the morning of September 11 his heart stopped and he died. He was just 49 years old.

Markov's dissident profile and the history of death threats made against him immediately alerted the authorities to the possibility of assassination, and his corpse was sent for a forensic autopsy, which found suggestive signs including hemorrhaging of the intestines, heart, and lymph nodes as well as a hugely elevated white blood cell count. The examination of Markov's body also found a tiny puncture wound on his right thigh with inflamed tissue surrounding it, and a tissue sample from the area was sent to the British government's Porton Down Chemical Defence Establishment Laboratory, where a tiny pellet was recovered. About the size of the head of a pin, it was recognized as being a jeweler's watch ball-bearing, but one which had been specially modified by the drilling of two tiny holes. These two holes connected to form an X-shaped well, making the tiny ball-bearing capable of storing a minute quantity of an as yet unknown but absolutely deadly substance.

The experts suspected that the pellet had originally been coated with wax, which would have sealed the unknown substance in place but melted once exposed to the heat of the human body, releasing its deadly cargo. But any wax that had existed must have melted and dispersed, for none was found on the pellet or in the wound. The investigators caught a break, however, for just two weeks before Markov's killing another exiled Bulgarian, Vladimir Kostov, had come perilously close to sharing his fate. Leaving a Paris Metro station Kostov had felt a sting, and the next day had been hospitalized with a high fever. Fortunately he recovered, and when the British detectives on the case heard of the incident they were able to examine him, locate his wound, and recover a tiny pellet just like the one found in Markov—except that this time some of the wax coating remained.

Circumstantial Evidence

What was contained in the tiny pellet found in Markov's leg, and how had it got there? There was no trace of any substance and toxicology tests on the dead man also came back negative. This in itself eliminated a number of potential toxins, and almost from the start, Christopher C. Green, the medical doctor and CIA expert called in to advise, suspected that ricin might be involved. It was known to have been the subject of intensive Soviet biological weapons research, and it matched Markov's terrible symptoms and the pathology detected by the autopsy, especially the hemorrhaging of the lymph nodes and internal organs, the localized inflammation around the puncture wound, and the high white cell count.

To further test their hypothesis investigators injected a pig—a common test animal as its physiology is similar to a human's—with ricin, which soon showed similar symptoms, including a fever and high white cell count. The pig was dead within 24 hours and an autopsy showed the same pattern of damage that had been found in Markov's body. So although it was impossible to prove definitively that ricin was the assassin's weapon, the circumstantial evi-

RICIN

Source:
Castor bean

Form:
Powder, pellet, aerosol, or solution

Antidote:
None

Overview

Ricin is found in the castor bean, a plant commonly grown for castor oil extraction. The mash left after oil has been extracted from the beans can be up to 5 percent ricin, and this can be isolated and purified relatively easily. These characteristics made ricin superficially attractive as a potential chemical weapon, and it is claimed that the U.S., during World War I, and the U.K. during the 1940s, both attempted to develop ricin weapons, including bombs that would create aerosols and ricin-coated bullets. In practice, however, ricin is not particularly suitable as a bio-weapon. It must be inhaled or ingested to work, meaning that relatively large quantities would be needed to produce effective casualty rates, and it is relatively easily denatured (biologically inactivated) by heat over 176°F (80°C). Despite this, modern-day terrorist groups have tried to synthesize ricin, presumably attracted by its ease of manufacture.

Symptoms

Ricin consists of two proteins—one opens a channel in cell membranes through which the other can pass, where it disrupts protein production and causes cell death. If enough cells die, lesions and hemorrhages appear, and eventually organs cease to function, leading to death. Symptoms depend on the type of exposure. Ingestion causes nausea, vomiting, diarrhea, gastric and intestinal bleeding, and shock, and can cause death within three to five days. Inhalation causes irritation and bleeding of airways and lungs, leading to weakness and fever, followed by lesions, fluid build-up, and respiratory failure. Injection causes localized tissue damage and also fever, nausea, widespread lesions, and hemorrhaging, leading to organ failure and death.

Treatment

One reason why ricin is so attractive to assassins is that there is no antitoxin and no effective treatment. Symptoms may be treated, and in the case of ingestion the patient may be given activated charcoal and/or have their stomach pumped. Recently, new methods for detecting ricin have been developed, and trials of vaccines are underway, but vaccination is preventative not curative.

FAMOUS CASES

Georgi Markov
(1929–78)

dence pointed to it, and in January 1979 the coroner's court in London ruled that Markov had been murdered with 450 micrograms of the poison.

Circumstantial evidence also suggested the use of an unusual delivery device for the poisoned pellet. Its lack of deformation, the small size of the hole in Markov's jeans, and the absence of powder burns all suggested something other than a conventional firearm. Instead it was thought that a compressed-air or spring-loaded device might have been used. Combined with the victim's own account, this supplied the final piece of the puzzle, and the investigators speculated that the umbrella Markov had been wounded by concealed a compressed-air gun, with a cylinder of air activated by a trigger in the handle, which would shoot the pellet out of a hole in the point. Intelligence analysts pointed the finger of suspicion at the notorious secret KGB laboratory Kamera—"the Chamber"—as the likely source of the slaughterous sunshade.

Agent Piccadilly

The identity of the assassin remained a much harder puzzle to crack. Investigators had hoped that the opening of state files in Bulgaria after the fall of the Iron Curtain in 1989 would reveal his name, and perhaps even lead to the perpetrator's prosecution, but the country preferred to turn its back on this dark chapter from its past.

Although Markov was posthumously pardoned for his "crimes," senior officials colluded to cover up the truth about his assassination, destroying masses of papers relating to the case. In 1992 a former Bulgarian intelligence chief was sent to jail for his part in the whitewash, while another senior official committed suicide before his case came to trial. Then in 2000 the Bulgarian government apparently drew a line under the issue by officially closing the case, but a Bulgarian journalist named Hristo Hristov persevered in an exhaustive search of the state archives. Finally, in 2005, he claimed to have identified the elusive umbrella assassin as a Danish man of Italian origin named Francesco Gullino, who was commissioned to "neutralize" Markov on the orders of the Durzhavna Sigurnost, the Bulgarian secret service, in an operation sanctioned by Todor Zhivkov himself.

According to the archives, Gullino had been caught smuggling on the Bulgarian border in 1970, and in return for his freedom had become an agent of the Bulgarian security services, working under the codename Agent Piccadilly. Posing as an antiques salesman Gullino had traveled to London three times in 1977 and 1978, on the last occasion leaving on the day that Markov was injected with the deadly pellet. It even transpired that British police had made the same discovery as Hristov, only 12 years earlier, for in 1993 Gullino was detained in Copenhagen and questioned about the murder. For reasons that are still not clear, however, he was released for lack of evidence and has since disappeared.

The parallels with the more recent Litvinenko case (see pp. 136–9) are all to clear to be ignored—an émigré dissident who presents a minor irritation is murdered with poison by an assassin whose identity is thought to be known, but who escapes justice.

Georgi Markov, the Bulgarian journalist and dissident murdered in 1978.

The pellet that killed Markov: a jeweler's watch ball-bearing modified by drilling two holes that connect to create a well.

ALEXANDER LITVINENKO

One of the most shocking assassinations of recent years involves a web of accusations, grudges, and exposés, bound together by a trail of radioactive poison that leads from London to Moscow, but, as yet, to no answers.

Alexander Litvinenko was a former officer of the FSB claiming political asylum in Britain, from where he accused the Russian leader Vladimir Putin of having orchestrated the 1999 Russian apartment bombings. This string of atrocities, blamed on Chechen rebels, was the pretext for a massive assault on the secessionist enclave of Chechnya, a war that boosted Putin's popularity as the new strong man of Russian politics. Litvinenko also accused Putin of being behind other terrorist incidents and the murder of Russian journalist Anna Politkovskaya—who was shot, but only after an earlier attempt to poison her had failed. In London Litvinenko found a powerful protector in the form of Boris Berezovsky, an exiled Russian billionaire and Putin's nemesis.

On November 1, 2006, Litvinenko fell ill. Initially he exhibited symptoms of severe food poisoning, but as his white blood cell count plummeted and his hair began to fall out, it became obvious he had been dosed with something horrible. Tests suggested traces of thallium, but treatment for this had no effect. Over the next three weeks Litvinenko deteriorated rapidly, while doctors struggled to work out what was killing him. On November 20 he was moved into intensive care, and three days later he died, but not before making one last accusation: "You may succeed in silencing one man but the howl of protest from around the world will reverberate, Mr. Putin, in your ears for the rest of your life."

Litvinenko and the people around him believed that he had been silenced by an FSB operation at the instigation of Putin, to punish him for getting too close to uncovering the "coup" that had brought Putin to power. Litvinenko's symptoms suggested radiation poisoning, and radioactive thallium was considered, recalling the 1955 Nikolay Khokhlov case (see

p. 128), but scientists failed to detect any gamma rays, the form of radiation associated with such cases. Just hours before his death, the Russian was tested with special equipment that could detect alpha radiation, a form in which highly destructive but relatively low-energy particles are given off: the particles do immense damage to anything in their immediate proximity, but cannot travel far—they can be stopped by just a piece of paper.

An autopsy on the body revealed that the source of the alpha radiation was polonium-210, so toxic that less than a milligram can kill within 20 days, according to the Health Physics Society. The levels of this rare radioactive substance in Litvinenko's body were so great that supposedly orders have been given that his coffin is not to be opened for seven years, or 22 according to some sources. In order for the alpha radiation to have killed him, the Russian must have ingested it, and the autopsy also suggested that he had been given two separate doses.

The Polonium Trail

Was the choice of this exotic poison inspired or stupid? On the one hand, polonium is so rare that once identified it can easily be traced—it almost certainly came from government-controlled Russian labs—and it leaves a blazing trail of contamination that is easy to follow once you know what you are looking for. On the other, however, it seems ideal: unlike most radioactive materials it can be easily smuggled through airports undetected in a vial of water, since the glass will contain the deadly alpha radiation; it is deadly, but symptoms take long enough to develop for the assassin to escape; and crucially, this appeared to be the first time polonium had ever been used to poison someone—although journalist Martin Sixsmith claims that former Putin bodyguard Roman Tsepov may also have been a victim of polonium in 2004. In the unlikely event that an alpha-radiation source was suspected, it should have been impossible to identify, and it nearly was—but, perhaps unbeknown to the assassins, the West does possess the ability to detect and identify polonium.

But for this, the cause of Litvinenko's death would have remained a mystery and no one would have known to search for the trail of radiation that might point to the assassin. However, once they knew what to look for, investigators were able to establish that he was probably poisoned at the Millennium Hotel bar, where he had met with two former KGB officers, Andrei Lugovoi and Dmitri Kovtun. From there the trail led to a sushi restaurant and lunch with Italian lawyer Mario Scaramella, who supposedly handed over information pertaining to the death of Politkovskaya.

Litvinenko left a trail of poison wherever he went, and contaminated everyone with whom he came into contact—although both his wife and Scaramella showed high levels of contamination, neither needed treatment. Meanwhile Lugovoi and Kovtun seemed to have left radiation trails of their own, including on planes, with distinctive characteristics showing that they had not been contaminated by the victim. The case against the Russian pair was growing, and it began to look as if at least one of them had brought the polonium to England and slipped it into the victim's tea. Then, in the first of many twists in the case, it was reported that Kovtun had been taken ill and fallen into a coma, from which he has since recovered.

Meanwhile, the British police were building up a case against Lugovoi, reportedly fingered as his killer by Litvinenko himself, just before he died. But on his return to Russia he was soon elected to the Russian parliament, conveniently rendering him immune from prosecution. The Russian government and Lugovoi himself have since angrily dismissed calls for his extradition.

Discovered in 1898 by Marie Curie and her husband, Pierre, polonium is a soft, silvery-grey radioactive metalloid that exists in many forms as unstable radioisotopes. It is found in uranium ores such as pitchblende (shown right) and can be obtained either from mining the ores or by chemically separating it from radium-226 in a nuclear lab. Polonium is so rare that only about 3.5 oz (100 g) is produced each year.

Smoke and Mirrors

The affair became increasingly murky. It was suggested that Litvinenko and Berezovsky had fallen out. Scaramella was deemed to be a highly suspicious figure. Litvinenko was accused of having been involved in smuggling nuclear materials—perhaps he had poisoned himself? Questions were asked about why he was meeting with the Russians in the first place. There were tales of shadowy fourth and fifth men dubbed Igor the Assassin and Vladislav. Litvinenko's own history and character were called into question, with stories suggesting he may have been part of Russian death squads in Chechnya. The *Daily Mail* reported that he was on the payroll of British security service MI6.

Journalist Martin Sixsmith launched his own investigation of the affair and arrived at a fiendishly complex tale, recounted in his 2007 book *The Litvinenko File*. In his account, Litvinenko had been a loyal footsoldier in the post-Soviet secret security apparatus, but had become increasingly disillusioned by the blurring of the lines between the state, private enterprise, and the criminal underworld. Assigned to an elite hit squad tasked with extrajudicial killings of underworld figures beyond the reach of the law, he had learned that his immediate boss was corrupt. He alerted superiors but nothing came of it, and when he was part of a group sent to kill Berezovsky, he instead warned the billionaire of the plot and the two became friends.

According to Sixsmith, Litvinenko's fatal move had been to railroad his colleagues into appearing with him at a press conference in which he made public his accusations. These men bore grudges, and Sixsmith suggests they convinced or coerced Lugovoi into helping them set up the assassination by making contact with Litvinenko to discuss potential business opportunities.

Without access to state facilities, and possibly Kamera itself, it is difficult to explain how the assassins acquired polonium; and it remains unclear to what extent FSB-related operatives are under the control of the central government. Analysts describe post-Soviet Russian power politics as a complex affair involving factions that cut across traditional divides between government, business, and the underworld. If Litvinenko was killed by one of these factions, he may well be another on the long roster of Kamera's victims.

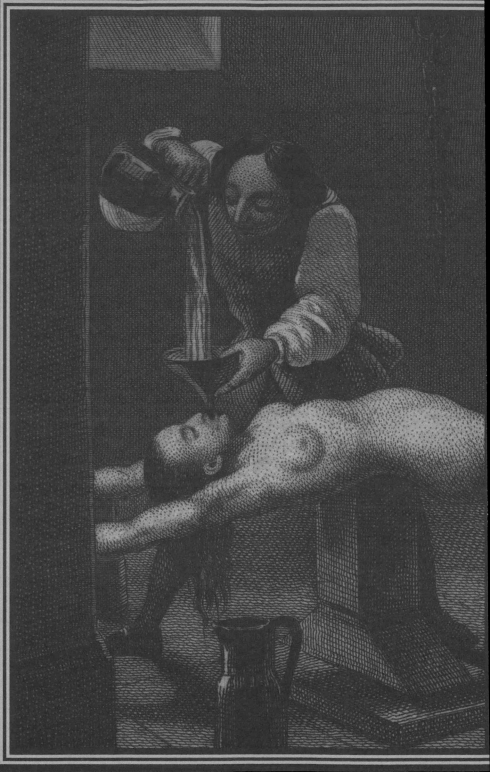

CHAPTER SIX

POISON

IN

MURDER

> "I love the old way best, the simple way of poison,
> where we too are strong as men."
>
> Euripides (c. 480–406 BC), *Medea*

MURDER BY POISON IS NOW SO RARE THAT IT MAKES GLOBAL HEADLINES, AS IN THE CASE OF ALEXANDER LITVINENKO, RECOUNTED IN THE PREVIOUS CHAPTER. BUT IN FORMER CENTURIES POISON WAS A MUCH MORE POPULAR TOOL FOR MURDER, AS THE MANY ACCOUNTS IN THIS CHAPTER SHOW. IS THIS SIMPLY A CASE OF CHANGING FASHIONS—IS THE PERNICIOUS ART OF MURDER AS SUSCEPTIBLE TO THE WHIMS OF TASTE AS HEMLINES OR HAIR LENGTHS?

In fact it probably has far more to do with practicality, for the modern era has seen many poisons, such as arsenic and cyanide, which were once freely available over the counter, become highly controlled substances; while science has also made great strides in the identification of poisons, and it is often possible to say exactly where one came from. Together, these developments mean that poison is now, in many ways, the worst choice for a calculating murderer.

However, a fascination with poison as a cold-blooded killer's weapon persists. Not least, for a number of reasons, when the poisoner is a woman. Female poisoners have been infamous since ancient times, while the Victorian era saw a glut of sensationalized cases reported in newspapers that were, then as now, hungry for salacious content. Female poisoners, with their titillating narratives, fed this appetite, and the disproportionate attention lavished upon them is reflected in the balance of the tales that make up this chapter. In reality, poisonings by either gender are rare in the modern era, but you can expect the next female poisoner to generate just as many headlines as her Victorian counterparts.

THE AFFAIR OF THE POISONS

Seventeenth-century Italy had seen a rash of murders by poison, ascribed to the evil influences of old women marketing easily available *poudres de succession*—arsenical poisons that disposed of unwanted husbands or relatives (see p. 80). This "mania for poisoning," as Charles Mackay described it, spread to France, culminating in a notorious episode known as L'Affaire des Poisons.

The first protagonist of this grim drama was the beautiful Marie d'Aubray, Madame de Brinvilliers. A young noblewoman who wished to dispose of her much older husband, she fell in with a rogue named Gaudin de Sainte-Croix, who had learned the recipe for a potent mix of arsenic and corrosive sublimate (mercury chloride) from a pharmacist named Glaser. Like many murderesses she was accused of testing her concoctions on the poor under the guise of charity.

Having perfected her dark arts, she used the potion to dispose of her father, husband, and several others, but was found out when Glaser was overcome by fumes from his own poison, and packets of it addressed to Madame de Brinvilliers were discovered alongside his body. She was executed in 1676 in grisly fashion; some accounts have her first being tortured with the "water cure"—being forced to drink a vast quantity of water—before being beheaded and burned at the stake.

The Witch la Voisin

The affair caused such a scandal that Louis XIV established a special commission to look into the problem of poisoning, the *Chambre Ardente*—"Burning Chamber." Uncovering the apparently rampant use of inheritance powders, the Chamber traced much of the poison back to one Catherine Deshayes, widely known as la Voisin, who was said to dispense a potent brew of arsenic, aconite, belladonna, and opium.

A midwife and fortune-teller, she was accused of being a witch and having made a compact with the Devil, and of running an entire staff of perverted priests, apothecaries, and midwives. Among them was a chemist named Lesage who prepared arsenical cosmetics; and a friar and alchemist named Brother Gérard, who was said to have concocted an arsenic-laden soap, which, when used to clean wounds, would swiftly finish off the victim.

This was a period of witch-hunts and mass burnings, and lurid accusations were made against la Voisin and her upper-class clientele, of whom she had helpfully kept a list. The Marshal de Luxembourg, a grand old man, was among the names, and according to eighteenth-century historian Lord John Russell, "The miserable gang who dealt in poison and prophecy alleged that he had sold himself to the Devil, and that a young girl of the name of Dupin had been poisoned by his means. Among other stories, they said he had made a contract with the Devil, in order to marry his son to the daughter of the Marquis of Louvois." The marshal protested his innocence but was confined in a cell just 6½ ft long for the duration of a 14-month-long trial.

Other notable persons said to be clients of la Voisin included the infamous and disreputable Duke of Buckingham and, most controversially, the king's mistress the Marquise de Montespan. Under interrogation la Voisin claimed that the marquise had purchased from her aphrodisiacs, and that together they had performed occult rites to help secure the favors of the king, including allowing a priest to perform a black mass over her naked body, at which a child was sacrificed. Although there was little hard evidence against the marquise, the scandal eventually forced her to retire to a convent.

La Voisin was horribly executed: burned alive in the center of Paris on February 22, 1680, after her hands had been bored through with a red-hot iron and then cut off. Meanwhile the Chamber continued its work, eventually executing 34 people—although Mackay contends that more than a hundred people were killed in the ensuing witch-hunt. The king was appalled at the scale of a scandal that threatened to undermine his rule, and in 1682 suppressed the investigation, sparing many aristocrats from trial and prompting the Chamber's head, Louis' chief of police Gabriel Nicolas de la Reynie, to observe that "the enormity of their crimes proved their safeguard."

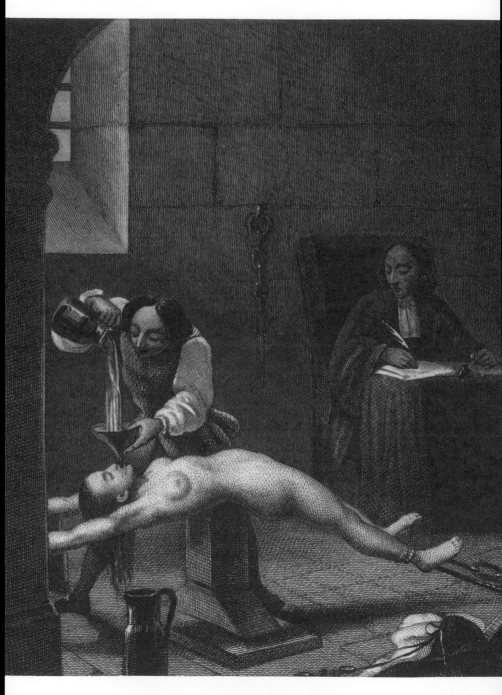

MARY ANN COTTON

One of England's most notorious mass murderers, Mary Ann Cotton operated under cover of the harsh conditions of working-class Victorian life. Terrible infant mortality rates, epidemic sudden death from gastrointestinal diseases, great mobility of people coupled with poor record keeping enabled her to kill as many as 20 people with impunity. Even when she was finally arrested, tried, and hanged, it remained uncertain exactly how many poisonings she had been responsible for.

Expendable Children

Born Mary Ann Robson to a coal-mining family in County Durham, England, in 1832, she was a bright and pretty girl who taught at Sunday school and worked as a nursemaid at one point. It was later alleged that this was where she had learned the art of poisoning; toxic materials were commonplace ingredients of medicines, pesticides, and cleaning products at this time. Arsenic soap, for instance, was used to wash down and disinfect bedposts.

In 1852 at the age of 19 she married a miner named William Mowbray. The couple moved to Cornwall, and this is where the string of suspect deaths connected with her began. Mary Ann had four children but three of them died suddenly of what was known as gastric fever—a catch-all term that covered several diseases characterized by gastrointestinal symptoms, such as typhoid fever. Spread by contaminated water and poor sanitation, such illnesses could indeed take hold and kill extremely quickly, especially in infants, but they also shared symptoms with arsenic poisoning.

An illustration of Madame de Brinvilliers under torture, published in an 1847 edition of *Crimes Célèbres* by Alexandre Dumas. The "water cure" involved forcing the victim to drink until her innards distended and burst.

After the Mowbrays returned to Country Durham in 1856 their fourth child also died of gastric fever. Four more children followed, but two of them died. Then in 1863, not long after William Mowbray had taken out life insurance, another child died, and when Mowbray himself fell ill and was unable to bring in a wage, he too perished, earning Mary Ann a tidy insurance payout. She needed the money, it was later said, for she was indolent and self-indulgent, employing others to do her housework—strange, you might think, for someone living on the breadline.

Mary Ann took a new lover, Joseph Natrass, but was still encumbered with two of Mowbray's children. However, one conveniently died and she dumped the other on her mother. The relationship with Natrass did not work out, and soon she was married to a George Ward. A year later he lost his job and shortly after that his life, succumbing to severe vomiting and diarrhea in 1866. Obtaining a job with widower James Robinson, Mary Ann quickly started sleeping with him. One of his five children died a week after she moved in.

In March 1867 she was called away to nurse her sick mother, who did not linger long, and the child she had been caring for died of gastric fever shortly after. In August of that year Mary Ann married Robinson. They had two children together, one of whom soon died, and in 1869 Robinson kicked her out. He had discovered her stealing from him, and according to some accounts had grown suspicious of her when she suggested he might take out some life insurance. Perhaps rewarded for his suspicions, Robinson was one of the few people involved with Mary Ann to survive.

"I Won't Be Troubled Long"

Mary Ann moved away and used forged references to obtain housekeeping positions, eventually hooking up with another widower with children, Frederick Cotton. She soon fell pregnant and the pair were married—albeit bigamously—in 1870. After suspicion fell on Mary Ann over the death of some pigs, the couple were forced to move on. They came to live on the same street as Mary Ann's former lover Natrass, and in September 1871 Cotton helpfully died so that the two of them could move in together and resume their relationship.

Perhaps because he could not support her in style, Natrass did not last long either, perishing along with two of the children Mary Ann had picked up from her marriage to Cotton.

This femme fatale then found a wealthier man, an excise officer named Quick-Manning, but he declined to marry her. She blamed Cotton's only surviving offspring, seven-year-old Charles Edward, and tried fostering him out and shipping him off to the workhouse. Told that they would not take him, she responded, "It won't matter, I won't be troubled long." And when the boy died a week later on July 12, 1872, officials became suspicious and reported her to the police, who in turn alerted the local doctor. He refused to issue a death certificate and carried out an autopsy on poor Charles. When he later subjected the boy's organs to a Reinsch test he found arsenic.

Mary Ann was arrested and charged with murder. The bodies of others associated with her were disinterred and also tested positive for arsenic. It also emerged that a few weeks previously she had purchased arsenic soap. The weight of evidence told against her and despite her defense that arsenic fumes from green wallpaper were the true culprit, she was found guilty of murdering Charles Edward and hanged on March 24, 1873.

The newspapers portrayed her as a black-hearted murderess, and although their coverage was almost certainly biased—her pretty features were deliberately coarsened in pictures—it is hard to disagree. It is impossible to know how many of the 20 or more deaths associated with her were actually due to poisoning, and how many genuinely were due to gastric fever or other causes of death common at the time; but it must be said that many of them were suspiciously convenient.

Although Mary Ann's deeper motives—if indeed there were any— remain hidden, the whole case paints a grim and disturbing picture of an era when children were considered to be expendable and of a woman who treated her own with shocking contempt.

THE RIPPER POISONINGS

A murderer who believed he had found the perfect, undetectable poison, George Chapman came to be known as the Borough Poisoner of Southwark, but is most notable as a strong suspect in the Jack the Ripper murders.

Chapman's real name was Severin Klosowski, and he was born and brought up in Poland where he trained as a barber-surgeon in Warsaw. In early 1888, at the age of 22, he emigrated to London, leaving behind a woman and two children. And it was the autumn of that year which saw London's East End terrorized by a series of six brutal and grisly murders, the first of which took place next door to Chapman's basement barber shop in Whitechapel.

Klosowski was high on the list of suspects, thanks to Inspector Abberline of Scotland Yard, who led the Ripper investigation, and came to suspect that, with his surgeon's skills and later record of murder, the Pole was the prime candidate. When Klosowski/Chapman was eventually convicted in 1903 Abberline supposedly remarked to the arresting officer, "You've got Jack the Ripper at last!"

It's interesting to note that the Ripper murders started at the same time as Klosowski's arrival, while there was a gap between the killings that coincided with his brief emigration to America. On the other hand, witness descriptions of the Ripper describe a much older man, with a polished English accent, and on top of this criminologists see a major difference between the modus operandi of a crazed mutilator and the calculating poisoner Klosowski turned out to be.

Fake Wives, Real Murder

An attractive man with a commanding manner, Klosowski fell into a pattern of sham marriages, presumably so that he could exercise his powerful sex drive amid the censorious mores of Victorian society. His first target was a young

Polish woman called Lucy, and after a period of fake marriage the two actually did get hitched, probably bigamously. They had children and tried emigrating to America, but quarrelled over his philandering, prompting him to become violent and threaten to kill her. Eventually they separated, although as they were Catholics they did not divorce.

In 1893 he took up with a woman called Annie Chapman, and although he soon left her he called himself George Chapman from then on. Then, in 1895, he met an older woman, Mary Spink, and the two pretended to get married. Chapman used her inheritance to buy a barber's shop by the sea, and later a pub in London. By 1897, however, he had tired of her drinking and went to a pharmacist to purchase an ounce of tartar emetic (potassium antimony tartrate). In November of that year Spink fell gravely ill, and by December she needed continuous nursing, suffering from constant vomiting, especially when Chapman gave her medicinal brandy, from a bottle he insisted was reserved strictly for her.

After a month of diarrhea, vomiting, and agonizing abdominal pains Spink's body could take no more and she died on Christmas morning. When her body was disinterred seven years later it was remarkably well preserved because it was saturated with antimony and had been so badly dehydrated at death. The unfortunate Mary Spink had died a torturous death from chronic poisoning by antimony administered over a period of many weeks.

Soon after her death, a woman called Bessie Taylor moved into the pub and she and Chapman pretended to get married. Then in 1899 the two of them moved to a new pub in Southwark, but they had been arguing violently and in late 1900 she fell ill, with similar symptoms to those suffered by Spink. This time a number of doctors were involved in her treatment, arriving at a variety of diagnoses. But it was only when her mother came down to London to nurse her that she began to recover, presumably because with Mrs. Taylor in constant attendance Chapman was now unable to slip her regular small doses of antimony. Thwarted in this way, he resorted to giving her a single massive dose, which duly killed her in the early hours of February 13, 1901. Again the attending doctor failed to spot the poisoning; but again, when the body was dug up nearly two years later, it proved to be remarkably well preserved. The bowels were coated with yellow antimony sulfide, produced from the reaction of antimony with the decomposition gas hydrogen sulfide, and her intestines were found to contain 548 mg of antimony, the largest quantity ever recorded in a murder victim.

"Fifty Doctors Would Not Find Out"

Chapman recovered from his grief quickly enough to reopen the pub that very same day, and it did not take him long to recruit a new, pretty young barmaid named Maud Marsh. Sure enough, in October 1901 he engaged in yet another sham marriage—the two of them got dressed in their finest, went to church and came back proclaiming themselves wed—but within a year his attentions shifted to another new barmaid and he began to poison his latest "bride." Maud was in and out of hospital with the characteristic symptoms of vomiting and abdominal pains, but once again none of the doctors who treated her suspected poisoning. Chapman was proud of continually outwitting the medical professionals, boasting to a customer that he could kill someone with a pinch of poison "and 50 doctors would not find out."

But this time he would not escape detection. Maud's father visited and became suspicious when Chapman kept insisting on personally supervising her meals and medicine. On October 21, 1902, Mr. Marsh remarked that she seemed to be getting better, only for Chapman to warn darkly, "She will never get up no more." The next morning he brought Maud some brandy and her condition worsened. Her mother, who was nursing her, also tried the brandy and was immediately stricken with vomiting and diarrhea.

When Maud died later the same day the family insisted on an autopsy and warned the police of their suspicions, and although Chapman tried to cover his tracks by disposing of his antimony and burning the sickroom sheets, he was arrested on October 25. Analysis of Maud's organs showed high levels of antimony and the police ordered the disinterment and testing of the corpses of Spink and Taylor. Chapman's fate was sealed. In a perfunctory trial he was found guilty of murder and hanged on April 7, 1903.

ANTIMONY

Source:
Stibnite and
tetrahedrite ores;
recycled from
lead-acid batteries

Form:
Pure element: bright,
silvery, hard metal;
tartrate: faint yellow
crystals

Antidote:
Dimercaprol

Overview

Antimony is a semimetal similar to arsenic. Although its mechanism of toxicity is unclear, it is believed to involve binding to sulfur-containing groups in many proteins—in other words, a similar mechanism to arsenic. The primary ore of antimony, black stibnite, has long been used as a medicine and cosmetic; the Romans called it *stibium*, from which the chemical symbol, Sb, derives. Medieval alchemists isolated the element itself, calling it *lupus metallorum*, the wolf of metals, and it was a key ingredient of alchemical recipes. One of the forms alchemists strove to create was a star-shaped crystal known as a *regulus*, which is credited with helping to inspire Newton's theory of gravity.

The form of antimony most commonly implicated in poisoning has traditionally been tartar emetic, the popular name for potassium antimony tartrate, which is widely used as a medicine. Antimony-containing medicines have been blamed for causing the death of Mozart. He was said to have died of a condition known as miliary fever, which was the name given to a constellation of symptoms similar to antimony poisoning, and it is known that he was being treated for "melancholia," for which antimony powders were a common treatment. Did he accidentally overdose on toxic medicine?

Symptoms

Antimony poisoning causes sweating, vomiting, nausea, stomach cramps, inability to retain food, loss of appetite, wasting, extreme dehydration, and great thirst.

Treatment

Chelation therapy using dimercaprol is highly effective, but to some extent antimony is its own best antidote because it causes violent vomiting that tends to clear the poison out of the stomach.

FAMOUS CASES

George Chapman
(1868–1903)

Wolfgang Mozart
(1756–91)

William Palmer
(1824–56)

Edward Pritchard
(1825–65)

Florence Bravo
(1845–76)

FLORENCE MAYBRICK

One of the most famous arsenic-poisoning trials of the Victorian era was that of Florence Maybrick, a beautiful American girl who married a British man some 23 years her senior. Young Florence met shipping broker James Maybrick on a liner traveling to Britain when she was just 17; they were married a year later in 1881 and soon moved to Liverpool. But what Florence did not know was that Maybrick already had a relationship with a shop girl who was eventually to bear him five children.

By 1887 he had fathered two more children with Florence, but their marriage foundered when she learned about his mistress. Florence soon found a lover of her own, 34-year-old Alfred Brierley. Things came to a head in 1889 when husband and wife began to quarrel openly, and he became violent. By that April the two appeared to reach an accommodation of sorts, but by then Florence was probably already plotting her husband's murder.

Cats and Flies Beware

Testimony at Florence's trial revealed that she had visited the pharmacy and bought a packet of black arsenic (arsenic trioxide mixed with soot to prevent it from being mistaken for food), labelled "Arsenic Poison" and "For Cats." Evidently she had claimed she needed it to poison some errant felines, who must have been persistent and sturdy beasts because she soon came back for a second packet. Florence also bought some arsenic flypapers, which, when soaked in water, released up to 400 mg of arsenic. She may well have learned about the toxicity of the flypapers from a notorious Liverpool murder of 1884 in which a pair of deadly sisters had employed them to dispatch four people.

Florence's plan, judging from the evidence at her trial, was to take advantage of her husband's hypochondria and his habit of dosing himself liberally with the potions and tonics of the day—fears about his flagging libido, for

Illustrations of Florence Maybrick and her abusive husband James, published in
The Graphic in 1869.

instance, prompted him to use Fowler's solution (see pp. 85–7), an arsenical
medicine that would prove significant. These patent medicines provided Florence with the cover for the arsenic solutions, which she prepared by soaking the
flypapers and filtering the black arsenic through a handkerchief.

James had been sent medicine by a doctor in London, but when he took
a double dose on Saturday, April 27, 1889 he became violently ill, with vomiting
and numbness of the extremities. No matter what he ate or drank for the rest of
the weekend he couldn't stop vomiting, but Florence had obviously misjudged
the lethal dose and by Monday he was on the mend. The next week she went out
and bought more flypapers, preparing more arsenic solution, which she slipped
into a special "invalid food" broth that James had been prescribed. On Friday,
May 3 he ate a whole jug, and it was this that most likely proved the fatal dose,
although Florence added smaller doses throughout the rest of the next week by
taking personal control of most of the food, drink, and medicine that was given
to him. Stricken with constant vomiting, diarrhea, pain, and weakness, James
took to his bed never to rise again.

A Horrible and Incredible Thought

Suspicions began to build against Florence, for she was observed in the act of pouring fluids from one bottle to another, and switching medicine bottles. At one point she asked a family friend to post an incriminating letter to her lover Brierley, but her supposed friend read it instead. On May 10, James uttered his last words: "Oh Bunny, Bunny, how could you do it? I did not think it of you." The next day he died. Searches of the house revealed poison secreted in Florence's room; she was put under house arrest, and a week later transferred to prison to await trial.

That July Florence's trial attracted huge interest from around the world. The sordid details of her love life and deadly plot titillated prurient Victorian audiences, but at the same time the shabby conduct and mismanagement of the trial provoked an international campaign to free her. Florence was seen as a martyr for women's rights because the trial revealed clear double standards in the moral conduct expected of men and women, and the judge's behavior added to calls for a Court of Appeal.

Florence's defense lawyer was the prosecutor from the Mary Ann Cotton case, and he employed the Styrian Defense (see pp. 87–9) to argue that James was an arsenic eater, and his consumption of arsenical medicines accounted for the amounts found in his body. Florence's possession of the arsenic solutions was explained away as being for purely cosmetic use.

The case for the prosecution was confusing and poorly presented, while the judge gave ample grounds for appeal by delivering an excoriating diatribe against the morals and character of Florence, opining that it was "a horrible and incredible thought that a woman should be plotting the death of her husband in order that she might be left to follow her own degrading vices."

Inevitably the jury found her guilty. She was sentenced to death but a public outcry saw this commuted to life imprisonment. The vociferous campaign for her release was outweighed by the enmity of Queen Victoria, who did not like what she had read of Mrs. Maybrick and whose disapprobation ensured that she served her full term of 15 years, before she returned to America where she lived to a ripe old age, dying in 1941 at age 79.

The Murder of Jane Stanford

Strychnine was the horrible poison at the center of one of the least-known but most successful murders of the twentieth century, the killing of Jane Stanford, co-founder of California's prestigious Stanford University. Born Jane Lathrop in Albany, New York, in 1828, she married Leland Stanford at the age of 20 and the two headed west, where Leland became a railroad tycoon. When they lost their only child to typhoid, the couple founded the university in his honor, and Jane became heavily involved in its running.

When Leland died in 1893 she became the University's sole trustee, devoting upon it "the commanding meddlesome love which an unbridled maternal instinct thrusts upon an only child," in the words of historians Richard Hofstadter and Walter P. Metzger. Her "meddling" extended to hiring and firing presidents and overseeing the day-to-day running of the institution. By 1905 she was engaged in an acrimonious falling-out with President David Starr Jordan, having become deeply suspicious of his ability to run her beloved college properly. She even had a spy inside the faculty, reporting to her on Jordan's actions, and was strongly considering deposing him.

A Horrible Death to Die

On the evening of January 14, 1905, Mrs. Stanford was at her mansion on Nob Hill, San Francisco's most exclusive district. As was her custom, she drank from a glass of mineral water that had been put out for her, just as it was every night. But even as she swallowed, she detected a strong bitter taste. Immediately she made herself sick. Did she perhaps suspect, even before the water had touched her lips, that her life was in danger? She then called for her secretary, Bertha Berner, who agreed that the water did not taste right. And indeed, when it was sent for analysis it proved to have been laced with a fatal dose of strychnine.

STRYCHNINE

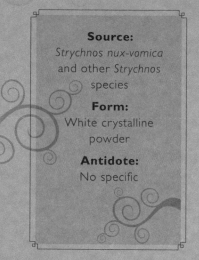

Source:
Strychnos nux-vomica
and other *Strychnos*
species

Form:
White crystalline
powder

Antidote:
No specific

Overview

Strychnine is a highly complex alkaloid, a class of organic chemicals distinguished by the presence of carbon rings and a nitrogen atom. The latter is responsible for the bitter taste of alkaloids, and strychnine is the most bitter of them all. In fact, it is the most bitter chemical known to man, and can be detected at concentrations of just eight parts in a million.

First isolated in 1817 from the St. Ignatius bean, a vine from the Philippines used as a medicine in China, it is commercially sourced from *Strychnos nux-vomica*, a medium-sized tree native to India. The seeds contain up to 1.4% strychnine, together with other alkaloids.

Strychnine acts on motor nerves in the spinal cord. It binds to and blocks (but does not activate) neuroreceptors for glycine. Normally these receptors are neuroinhibitory—that is, they help to regulate and limit the excitation of nerves. Blocking them removes this inhibition, so that the motor neurons fire in response to much lower levels of neurotransmitter. The slightest stimulation causes them to go haywire, with horrible effects for the sufferer.

Symptoms

Disinhibition of motor neurones causes violent convulsions of all muscles, which in turn leads to the tetanic spasm characteristic of strychnine poisoning. Because the muscles of the back are stronger than those of the front, the victim arches up on his or her heels and the top of the head. Death is caused by asphyxiation from spasms of the diaphragm and the thoracic and abdominal muscles. One of the most distressing features of death by strychnine poisoning is that the victim remains conscious until the end. Other symptoms caused by the same mechanism include nystagmus (rapid side-to-side movement of the eyes) and hyperthermia (overheating) from the intense muscle activity. If the victim survives the initial effects, muscle breakdown products can lead to kidney damage, while nerve-cell death can result in permanent damage even after recovery.

Treatment

There is no specific antidote, but therapy to limit the severity of convulsions can keep the victim alive until the poison is cleared from his or her system. This involves muscle relaxants, tranquillizers, and resting in a dark, quiet room with no stimuli.

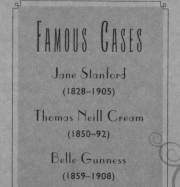

FAMOUS CASES

Jane Stanford
(1828–1905)

Thomas Neill Cream
(1850–92)

Belle Gunness
(1859–1908)

A month later Mrs. Stanford, her loyal secretary Berner in tow, set off for Hawaii for a dose of tropical sun. The pair checked into the Moana Hotel in Honolulu, and it was here, on the night of February 28, that Mrs. Stanford asked Berner to prepare her an *aide digestive*, in the form of a glass of bicarbonate of soda. A little while later the suite suddenly rang out with the sound of her anguished cries, "Run for the doctor! I have no control of my body! I think I have been poisoned again!"

A doctor was duly fetched—the hotel physician Dr. Francis Humphris— and on entering the room he found Mrs. Stanford in a state of extreme distress. Between spasms she managed to gasp, "My jaws are stiff. This is a horrible way to die." Indeed it was. Another convulsion took hold, described by Stanford professor Robert Cutler in his book *The Mysterious Death of Jane Stanford*: "Her jaws clamped shut, her thighs opened widely, her feet twisted inwards, her fingers and thumbs clenched into tight fists, and her head drew back. Finally, her respiration ceased."

The Cover-Up

Humphris and several other doctors did their best to save her, but to no effect. An autopsy and coroner's jury were ordered, and the jury quickly arrived at the conclusion that "Jane Lathrop Stanford came to her death ... from strychnine poisoning, said strychnine having been introduced into a bottle of bicarbonate of soda with felonious intent by some person or persons to this jury unknown."

Said person or persons remain unknown to this day, partly thanks to the immediate aftermath of the incident. Even as the coroner's inquest was in session, the university president Jordan was on his way out to Honolulu, apparently intent on hushing up a potential scandal. He hired a local doctor, Ernest Waterhouse, to produce his own report on Mrs. Stanford's death, and hastily announced to the press that the poor lady had died of heart failure. All talk of poisoning was nonsense, Jordan insisted, going to great lengths to rubbish the reputations of Humphris and the other doctors who had treated Mrs. Stanford, and even suggesting that Humphris had added strychnine to the bicarbonate bottle after Stanford's death in order to conceal his own incompetence. The poisoning was swept under the carpet, and to this day the official story is that there was no foul play involved.

In fact it was Waterhouse whose competence was suspect, and after receiving a large sum from Jordan he sailed for Ceylon (modern-day Sri Lanka). The autopsy, carried out by seven doctors and a toxicologist, was very clear about the cause of death, and Jordan must have known he was covering up the truth. Did he do it simply to protect the reputation of the university or did he murder Mrs. Stanford? He certainly seems to be the prime suspect, on account of the threat to his job, but did he have the opportunity? The only person present at both poisonings was Bertha Berner, but she was a loyal and well-loved companion of 30 years. Despite the fact that her loyalty was rewarded in Mrs. Stanford's will, which might constitute a motive, Berner was exonerated when questioned by police.

Over a century later there is no way to know who killed Jane Stanford, but Cutler's investigation has revealed that she definitely was poisoned with strychnine. Beyond that, all we can know for sure is that someone got away with murder.

Strychnos nux-vomica grows in India and parts of Southeast Asia. The seeds are flattened disks with a characteristic sheen imparted by a dense covering of satiny hairs. The plant is rich in toxic alkaloids, notably strychnine but also brucine, and has long been used for medicinal purposes. For instance, a tincture of the plant was used to stimulate peristalsis of the gut to treat constipation. A related species is *Strychnos toxifera*, the South American vine that yields curare.

THE INFAMOUS DR. CRIPPEN

Known as the North London Murder or the Cellar Murder, Dr. Crippen's dark deed was the most celebrated and notorious criminal story of its age. The house at the center of the mystery was, for a time, known as "the most famous house in London," and a waxwork of Dr. Crippen still resides in the Chamber of Horrors at Madame Tussaud's, the London waxwork museum. An enthralled public on both sides of the Atlantic heard a lurid tale of sex, betrayal, murder, gruesome dismemberment, cross-dressing, and a transatlantic chase triggered by the use of the latest technological marvel, the wireless telegram. But much about the Crippen case does not add up. Was the small, unassuming man at its center truly the most despicable fiend of the era? Why did he use such an unlikely poison to dispose of his victim? And have cutting-edge genetic technologies cleared his name, albeit nearly a century too late?

Belle and Belladonna

Hawley Harvey Crippen was always referred to as "Dr." because in the United States, the land of his birth, he was a qualified physician. In Britain, however, his diplomas did not allow him to practice medicine, and he scraped by on odd medical jobs, such as dentistry and patent-medicine sales, after moving to London in 1900 with his second wife, a woman of several names. Born Kunigunde Mackamotski, to Crippen she was Cora Turner, while to the music-hall fraternity with whom she was popular she was known as Belle Elmore, a singer of modest talent but voracious sexual appetites. When she openly cuckolded Crippen with a number of men, he responded by starting an affair with his one-time typist, Ethel le Neve.

By 1909 Crippen and Cora were living at 39 Hilldrop Crescent, a reasonably large house in north London. The rent here appears to have been beyond Crippen's paltry official earnings, and they probably let rooms to lodgers, but there was also evidence of other sources of income. The Crippens had more than £600 on deposit at the bank and Cora sported expensive jewelry and furs. It is widely speculated that "Dr." Crippen—as *The Times* newspaper would later insist on calling him—was an abortionist, an illegal practice at the time.

In December 1909 the relationship between Crippen and Cora seems to have broken down and she may have threatened to leave him and take their joint savings with her, because she gave notice of withdrawal to the bank. On January 19, 1910, according to testimony given at a later inquest, Crippen ordered from a pharmacist five grains (over 300 mg) of hyoscin hydrobromide, stating that he wanted it for homeopathic preparations.

Hyoscine, today better known as scopolamine, is a tropane alkaloid found in belladonna (see p. 52), henbane, and datura (see p. 51), amongst others. It has been used to treat motion sickness and nausea, for ophthalmic therapies and as a kind of anesthetic. Although it is extremely toxic, and Crippen had purchased many times the lethal dose, it seems like a peculiar choice for a murder weapon. It has been suggested that Crippen used it to sedate his wife before doing her in, or even that he believed it would douse her raging libido. Advocates of his innocence suggest that he intended it for use in his illegal abortions, or employed it legitimately in his work.

Cora Crippen seems to have disappeared on February 1, for that day Crippen pawned some of her jewelry and Ethel le Neve spent the night at 39 Hilldrop Crescent. Over the next few weeks Crippen tried to construct a convincing narrative for her disappearance. Letters signed "Belle Elmore" but in someone else's handwriting offered her resignation from the Music Hall Ladies Guild, of which she was Honorary Treasurer. Crippen span a story about her returning to America suddenly, and once she was there falling ill and dying from pneumonia. He also prevented the sending of memorials to her supposed place of death. Her friends became suspicious, especially when le Neve was seen openly wearing Cora's furs and jewelry, and accordingly they notified Scotland Yard.

A Gruesome Discovery

Chief Inspector Dew of the Yard called on the "doctor" at work and also visited Hilldrop Crescent. Eventually Crippen admitted he had lied, claiming instead that Cora had gone to Chicago to take up with one of her lovers, and Crippen had invented the tale of her death to avoid scandal. If he had left it at that, he would have gotten away with murder, for Dew found the tale convincing. But Crippen panicked, fleeing to Antwerp, accompanied by le Neve disguised as a boy. When Dew called again at Hilldrop Crescent he found it empty. Suspicious, he arranged for a search and on July 13 human remains were discovered, preserved in lime that was probably meant to have destroyed them—the lime had become wet and turned into slaked lime, a preservative.

The narrative that later emerged at the trial was that Crippen had poisoned his wife to death, and then dismembered and dissected her in an attempt to dispose of the remains. All that was left were the organs and

The unprepossessing Hawley Harvey Crippen, who became the most notorious killer of his era as the Cellar Murderer.

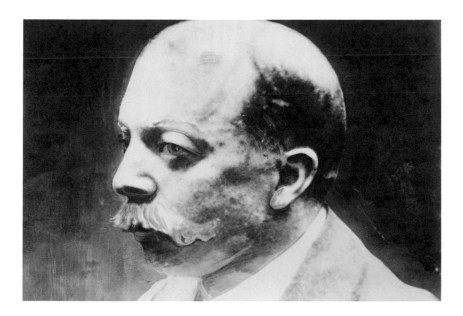

chunks of flesh. The limbs and skeleton, it was said, had been dissolved in a bath of acid, while the head was put in a bag and tossed over the side of a cross-Channel ferry. What was left was analyzed to reveal the presence of hyoscine, and identified as Cora from an old operation scar she was known to have on her abdomen. A pair of pajama bottoms buried with the remains helped prove they had been interred very recently, and Crippen happened to be missing just such an item. The case against him was overwhelming.

While all this was going on Crippen and le Neve had boarded the *Montrose*, en route from Antwerp to Canada, but the papers were full of the story and the ship's captain almost immediately spotted the pair and recognized Crippen as the supposed "Cellar Murderer." Using the new wireless telegram, he radioed back to shore to alert the authorities and Dew boarded the *Laurentic*, a faster ship than the *Montrose*. When the latter ship arrived he was there to meet it, introducing himself to Crippen who supposedly replied: "Thank God it's over. The suspense has been too great. I couldn't stand it any longer."

An Innocent Man?

The jury took less than half an hour to decide that Crippen was guilty. He was sentenced to death and on November 23, 1910—the same day that Le Neve, who had been cleared, sailed to America to start a new life—he was hanged. In 2007, however, an American team tested DNA from a preserved piece of the remains purported to be those of Cora Crippen, and compared them to DNA from a woman claiming to be her grand-niece. Not only did the analysis show that the two were not related, but the remains appeared to be those of a man.

But how seriously should claims of Crippen's innocence be taken? The recent genetic analysis may well be flawed. Such analyses should not be considered proven until replicated by other laboratories, and it seems unlikely that this will happen. The evidence against Crippen was damning, and considerably stronger than unprovable claims about perjuring policemen or the questionable psychology of poisoners. While today there might be grounds for appeal, there seems little doubt that Crippen murdered his wife and callously dissected her corpse.

THE TEACUP POISONER

Thallium was the toxin of choice for one of the most chillingly psychopathic poisoners in modern history, Graham Young. Young's early life story makes disturbing reading—he displayed all the classic warning signs of a serial killer in the making. His mother died of post-partum complications and he was sent to live with his aunt, but when his father remarried two years later Young was returned to him. The separation caused great distress to him; perhaps it was this that set him on the path to psychopathy?

Young Poisoner

Young grew up to be a strange, solitary child, obsessed with crime and murder, and particularly with Dr. Crippen (see pp. 161–4) and Hitler. He dabbled in the occult and probably killed a number of cats. He also developed a keen interest in chemistry, quickly outstripping the school curriculum. By age 14 his knowledge of toxicology enabled him to convince local pharmacies that he was much older, allowing him to get his hands on dangerous substances including antimony sodium tartrate, atropine, digitalis, aconite, and thallium acetate. He decided to test his burgeoning expertise on fellow pupil Christopher Williams, feeding him a cocktail of poisons that made him seriously ill, but was frustrated by the fact that he could not observe his victim's sufferings. Young resolved to test his skills closer to home, and set about poisoning his entire family.

In November 1961 he put atropine in his sister's teacup and was nearly discovered when she blamed him for her subsequent illness. Meanwhile he was already poisoning his stepmother, Molly, with regular small doses of antimony sodium tartrate. She suffered intermittent illness until April 20, 1962 when Graham slipped a large dose of thallium into her evening meal. The next day her husband found her writhing in agony while Graham looked on. She died later that night, her death misdiagnosed as a spinal-cord problem. Molly's cremation helped ensure that Graham evaded detection, while his father seems to have been unable to countenance the idea that Graham could be responsible, even when he too came down with attacks of vomiting and stomach cramps and was diagnosed with antimony poisoning.

Eventually Young was rumbled by a chemistry teacher who discovered that his school desk was full of poisons and alerted the police. The young poisoner was assessed by a psychiatrist, arrested, and sent to prison after admitting to some of his crimes—although not the murder of his step-mother. He was committed to Broadmoor—Britain's maximum-security prison for the criminally insane—as the third youngest inmate in its history.

Psychopaths are cunning and manipulative, and Young seems to have realized that if he ever wanted to be released he would have to fool the authorities that he was cured. In practice he was almost certainly still poisoning people. Soon after he arrived at Broadmoor a disturbed prisoner apparently committed suicide by cyanide, and it was rumored that Young had extracted the deadly substance from laurel bushes in the grounds. By 1971 he had convinced two psychiatrists that he was a reformed character, even as he warned a nurse that he intended to kill one person for every year of his incarceration.

The Toxic Tea Boy

After his release Young stayed at a hostel, where a fellow resident, Trevor Sparkes, soon suffered symptoms of poisoning. Meanwhile, another young man associated with Young was driven to suicide by painful attacks of illness. Young got a job at Hadland Laboratories in Bovingdon, a photographic processing company that was among the few firms in the country to legitimately use thallium. Initially one of his jobs was to make tea and coffee for the staff, and he took advantage of this to dose dozens of them with antimony and thallium. In particular he focused his attacks on his boss, Bob Egle, who suffered from cramps, dizziness, pain, and loss of sensation in his extremities. Egle was admitted to hospital and died on July 7, 1971.

By September so many Hadland employees were coming down sick that the local press dubbed the mystery illness "the Bovingdon Bug." Some employees suffered permanent damage, including impotence, while Young's co-worker Fred Biggs was afflicted worse than most. Suffering from similar symptoms to Egle, he died in great pain that November. The panicked staff were called together for a meeting to discuss the health issues, at which the company doctor admitted to being baffled. At this point Young stood up and asked whether thallium poisoning had been considered, showing off his toxicological knowledge. Suspicions were aroused, the police were alerted, and a long-overdue background check led to Young's arrest. A search of his rooms revealed a store of poisons and a diary recording details of his crimes, while post-mortem analyses revealed the presence of thallium in his victims.

In June 1972 Young was found guilty of murder and sentenced to four life terms. Incarcerated at Parkhurst maximum-security prison, he formed a close relationship with Moors Murderer Ian Brady, and the two spent much time discussing Hitler and the Nazis. Young even sported a Hitler mustache at times. He died on August 1, 1990, at the age of 42, officially of heart failure. His notoriety is said to have inspired subsequent uses of thallium as a poison, and in 1995 his life and dark deeds were turned into a film—*The Young Poisoner's Handbook*, perhaps appropriately, a black comedy.

Thallium was discovered almost simultaneously in 1861 by British scientist William Crookes and Frenchman Claude-Auguste Lamy—who identified a selenium-containing substance deposited during the production of sulfuric acid from pyrite (shown below)—although after a long and undignified tussle Crookes got most of the credit. He named the element for the bright green color it imparted to a flame when burned, deriving its name from the Greek *thallos*, meaning "green shoot."

CHAPTER SEVEN

POISON

IN

SUICIDE

"Let me have a dram of poison, such soon-speeding gear as will disperse itself through all the veins, that the life-weary taker may fall dead."

William Shakespeare (c. 1564–1616), *Romeo & Juliet*

OMEO'S HEART-BROKEN PLEA TO THE APOTHECARY ECHOES THE DESIRES OF WOULD-BE SUICIDES THROUGH HISTORY FOR AN END THAT IS QUICK, FINAL, AND HOPEFULLY PAINLESS. INDEED MUCH THE SAME RATIONALE SEEMS TO LIE BEHIND THE USE OF POISON AS AN AGENT OF SUICIDE AS FOR ITS EMPLOYMENT AS A MEANS OF EXECUTION: THE BELIEF THAT IT OFFERS A PEACEFUL, CERTAIN, HUMANE, CLEAN DEMISE—DEATH WITH DIGNITY. IN PRACTICE THESE BELIEFS ARE OFTEN MISPLACED.

Suicide by poison—including intentional drug overdoses, where the suicide intends to make use of the dose-dependent action of therapeutic drugs—has a relatively low success rate. Mistakes and ignorance also mean that suicides can experience far more pain than they expected. Many poisons, for instance, cause liver damage, which can be agonizing. Acetaminophen—one of the commonest agents for self-harm—is the leading cause of acute liver failure in both the U.S. and U.K. Even those that kill relatively quickly, like cyanide (see p. 126), probably cause intense pain before death.

All of this, however, has done little to dampen enthusiasm for this mode of suicide. Poison is still key to a wide spectrum of suicides, both attempted and realized, and remains popular for such disparate ends as assisted suicides in the face of terminal illness on the one hand and self-immolating cults on the other. Presumably these modern-day counterparts of the poison suicides of yesteryear, such as Demosthenes and Cleopatra, also subscribe to the belief that poison is the panacea for life's pain.

Juliet Discovering Romeo's Body (1890) by Ludovico Marchetti. One of the most famous cases of suicide by poison. Juliet awakens to find that Romeo, unaware that her "death" was a drug-induced fake, has swallowed real poison.

DEMOSTHENES

The ancient Greeks and Romans were firm believers in suicide in the face of defeat and capture—not only was it the honorable option, it also spared them from potential torture and gruesome execution, and encouraged enemies to spare their families. One of the most celebrated instances of such a "glorious" suicide is that of Demosthenes, the celebrated orator and politician, whose death has acquired semi-legendary status thanks largely to his wit and sang-froid in the face of death.

Jaw-Jaw and War-War

Demosthenes was the epitome of the orator—the public speaker whose command of rhetoric stirred hearts and minds, won arguments, and destroyed enemies. The young man grew up, according to legend, with a stutter that made him shy and quiet, but he resolved to overcome it. And indeed his first public speech, at the age of 20, was a success.

His soaring rhetoric ensured that he would go on to become a successful lawyer and speechwriter, and gravitate towards politics. A fierce patriot who believed that his gift for oratory could help Athens recapture its glory days, he correctly foresaw that the greatest threat to his goal, and to Athenian independence, was the growing menace of Macedon to the north. Here the ruthless Macedonian king Philip II had united his homeland and embarked on an ambitious program of expansion. While his great rival, the politician Aeschines, argued that Athens could never overcome the Macedonian war machine, Demosthenes counseled against appeasement and insisted that Athens and the other Greek city-states should stand up to Philip, on the battlefield if necessary.

In practice Demosthenes' ambitions for Athens exceeded its military and financial capabilities; exhausted by many decades of conflict, the city-state was never able to oppose Phillip successfully, although it did manage to avoid being sacked and razed. Demosthenes tirelessly championed his views, fomented rebellions, proposed alliances, channeled money from the Persians, and generally caused trouble for the Macedonians.

Poison Pen

When Philip died Demosthenes opposed Philip's son Alexander, and then, in turn, Antipater, Alexander's successor in Greece. Antipater and Athens contested the brief Lamian War but, by early August 322 BCE, the rebellion was crushed. Antipater's condition for sparing Athens was that the faction that had opposed him—which included Demosthenes—should be surrendered to him. The Athenian Assembly had little choice but to condemn the men accordingly, so Demosthenes and the others fled, the famed orator taking refuge on the tiny island of Calauria, where an ancient temple to Poseidon offered sanctuary.

Antipater sent after him one of his lieutenants, an erstwhile actor named Archias, at the head of a unit of Thracian spearmen. When he arrived he surrounded the temple, but loath to defile its sanctity, he pleaded with the Athenian to come out of his own accord, promising that Antipater would pardon him. Demosthenes replied archly, "Archias, you never moved me by your acting, and you will not move me now by your promises." He did, however, promise to come out after he had written a last note to friends.

Moving into the inner sanctum of the temple he took out his pen and, as was his habit, chewed its end, apparently in thought. In fact the reed was full of poison, and Demosthenes covered his head with his cloak, threw back his head, and drank it. Archias was suspicious and came in to talk to him, but Demosthenes waited until he could feel the toxin's deadly effect before getting to his feet and tottering out of the temple, falling dead as he passed the altar.

What was the poison in Demosthenes' pen? The ancient sources give little clue as to symptoms, but it must have been potent and fast-acting. Perhaps it was an adapted form of the State Poison (see pp. 99–101), although this seems to have involved larger draughts than the one Demosthenes took. So, as Demosthenes' cool head and sharp tongue live on, the identity of the poison with which he made his final act of defiance is lost to the pages of history.

CLEOPATRA AND THE ASP

Perhaps the most famous suicide in history was supposedly accomplished by the application of a venomous snake. But even the primary sources for the legendary tale of Cleopatra and the deadly asp were sceptical, and almost every detail of the story is open to debate.

The Last Days

Cleopatra was the last ruler of the Ptolemaic line of pharaohs that traced itself back to Alexander's general Ptolemy. Her world was an exotic combination of Egyptian and Hellenistic influences, alien to the Romans who had come to dominate the Mediterranean world, but all the more appealing for it. A woman now believed to have been more striking than beautiful, she was immensely attractive as well as sophisticated, charming, intelligent, and highly educated. Having secured the favors of Julius Caesar—and borne him a son, Caesarion—she subsequently became the lover and ally of Mark Anthony.

Anthony had been Caesar's right-hand man, and after Caesar's assassination in 44 BCE had joined forces with the dictator's adopted son, Octavian—later Augustus. But once the empire had been secured, the two, almost inevitably, became enemies and engaged in a civil war that raged across the Eastern Mediterranean. Octavian's fleet overcame Anthony and Cleopatra's combined navies at the great battle of Actium in 31 BCE, and the pair returned to Alexandria, dispirited. Anthony's forces began to desert and by the time Octavian arrived in Egypt their final defeat was assured.

Cleopatra, fearing capture, fled to her mausoleum and sealed herself inside. When it was reported to Anthony that Cleopatra had committed suicide, he killed himself; but in fact she was very much alive and may even have sent the message herself to trick him into committing suicide in an attempt to curry favor with Octavian.

Cleopatra posed a problem for Octavian as the focus of opposition to his rule over Egypt; while for her part, Cleopatra feared being paraded in humiliation through Rome. However, Octavian worried that such a procession might simply evoke pity, and must also have been mindful that she had at one time been the consort of his adopted father, the source of his legitimacy. In other words she promised to cause Octavian trouble whether he let her live or had her killed.

A Beautiful Death

Against this complex background Cleopatra was given the opportunity to arrange things to her design. Although, by a ruse, she had been taken captive by Octavian's forces, she was allowed to stay in chambers in her own palace, with guards posted outside. On August 12, 30 BCE, she sent away all but two of her maidservants—and a eunuch, according to some of the sources—and arrayed herself in her finery. Her Hellenistic tradition meant that suicide was an honorable option, and she meant to carry it off in style.

When Octavian's messengers, alerted by a final note penned by the queen, opened the doors to her chamber they found her already dead. Graeco-Roman historian Plutarch described the scene:

> *"they saw her stone-dead, lying upon a bed of gold, set out in all her royal ornaments. Iras, one of her women, lay dying at her feet, and Charmion, just ready to fall, scarce able to hold up her head, was adjusting her mistress's diadem. And when one that came in said angrily, 'Was this well done of your lady, Charmion?' 'Extremely well,' she answered, 'and as became the descendant of so many kings.'"*

But exactly how did she die? Ancient sources are contradictory and some modern historians feel the traditional account does not add up. Cassius Dio recounts that the only marks on the queen were pricks on the arm, but what made them? Plutarch and Dio both repeat the story of a snake being smuggled to Cleopatra hidden in a jar of figs or water, although both were sceptical. The Greek Strabo, who may have been in Alexandria at the time, writes that her death was caused "by the bite of an asp or (for two accounts are given) by applying a poisonous ointment," and other options suggested include poison applied via a hairpin or a hollow comb, or, according to Galen, that she broke the skin by biting her arm. It's interesting to note that the popular image of Cleopatra being bitten on the breast seems to have been created by Shakespeare for dramatic purposes.

But why would Cleopatra choose snake poison at all? Supposedly, having tested a range of poisons on slaves, prisoners, and animals, she dismissed a host of better-known poisons in favor of the bite of the asp, which brought a sleepy, painless death without disfigurement or contortion.

In practice this seems highly unlikely. The symptoms simply don't fit, and it is hard to be sure that the snake would inject a sufficient dose. One

Alexandre Cabanel's 1887 painting *Cleopatra Testing Poison on Condemned Prisoners* depicts Cleopatra observing the effects of poison on prisoners, before supposedly choosing the bite of an asp as the agent of her own demise.

solution, suggested by several Classical writers, is that two snakes were used, but as we have already seen the ancient sources themselves suggest such alternatives as hairpins and hollow combs.

However, there is another possibility; one which points the finger at Octavian. Certainly he was keen to promote the asp of legend—including in his triumphal procession back in Rome an effigy of Cleopatra on her couch with a snake attached. In practice, the person who benefited most from this neat and tidy suicide was Octavian himself, and one simple solution to the mystery of how she died is that the future Augustus had her killed and covered up his deed with propaganda. Could the most famous suicide of all have been murder?

If Cleopatra's death was indeed suicide by snake, then what type of snake? "Asp" was a generic term in antiquity and covered a range of venomous snakes. In Europe, for instance, it probably referred to *Vipera aspis*, the European asp, but in an Egyptian context it is less clear which species it refers to. One possibility is the horned sand viper, *Cerastes cornuta*; another the closely related *Cerastes vipera*, also known as the Egyptian asp or even Cleopatra's asp. The most usual translation of "asp" in an Egyptian context, however, is the Egyptian cobra, *Naja haje* (shown left) and this would have been an appropriately symbolic choice, for the queen upon her deathbed wore a pharaonic headdress featuring the *uraeus*, a stylized cobra symbolic of sovereignty and sacred to the goddess Isis, of whom she believed herself to be an avatar.

DEATH-WISH NAZIS

The collapse of the Third Reich and imminent defeat in the Second World War signaled the end of the world for leading Nazis. At least five of the highest-ranking Nazis would commit suicide by cyanide—although some shot themselves at the same time to make certain of death. The strange and terrible tale of their last days seems to encapsulate something of the perverted, morbid spirit of Nazism, and it was fitting that poison should spell the end for those who did so much to poison history.

By the end of April 1945, Hitler and his crumbling command structure were eking out their final days in a bunker beneath the Reich Chancellery in the heart of Berlin. Russian armies were closing in around them, razing the city in a battle of apocalyptic proportions. On April 28 Hitler received news that his right-hand man Heinrich Himmler, the SS Reichsführer, had been trying to sue for peace with the Allies. This was the last straw for Hitler, who promptly began his final preparations. He issued a barrage of delusional orders nominating successors, dictated his last will and testament and got married to Eva Braun. The two enjoyed a quiet wedding meal with champagne. Meanwhile, upstairs in the surface levels of the bunker, the last days of the Reich had descended into a grotesque orgy of sex and drinking.

Two days later, Hitler decided that his time had come. According to the British historian Antony Beevor, in his epic account of the fall of the Third Reich, *Berlin: The Downfall, 1945*, "Hitler's … great preoccupation remained his fear of being taken alive by the Russians." He had been particularly affected by news of Mussolini's brutal death, underlining in a news report on the incident the words "hanged upside down." He was also concerned that capture and interrogation would somehow sully his historical record. Meanwhile, the latest news of the fighting confirmed that there would be no relief, and that they had two days or less before the Russians—who were by now within sight of the bunker—broke through.

His personal physician Dr. Ludwig Stumpfegger had given him ampoules of cyanide—these were standard issue to Nazis and consisted of small glass containers filled with prussic acid (hydrocyanic acid); they even came with brass cartridge-case holders. But Hitler was terrified they would not work properly. He decided to test them on his loyal German shepherd bitch Blondi, and her four puppies. They were taken up to the Reich Chancellery garden to be killed.

The experiment successful, Hitler summoned his personal adjutant and gave instructions for the disposal of his corpse and his wife's. He then ate lunch with his two secretaries and his dietician. A little later he and his wife made their farewells to the inner circle and went into their rooms. Guards were posted at the door.

Nobody heard the shot but Hitler is said to have bitten down on the cyanide ampoule and shot himself in the head at the same time. At 3:15 PM a number of people entered his sitting room to confirm that he was dead: His body was quickly covered in a blanket but curious onlookers could see that Eva Hitler's lips were puckered from the cyanide. The corpses were taken up the garden, drenched in petrol, and set alight. A watching SS guard called down to the others, "The chief's on fire. Do you want to come and have a look?"

Cyanide takes its name from the Greek *kuaneos*—"dark blue"—which reflects its discovery from the pigment Prussian blue, now made by adding iron chloride to potassium ferrocyanide (shown below).

Why did so many Nazis use cyanide capsules to end their lives? Perhaps because they were obsessed with technology, industralization, and modernism. The cyanide capsule, product of the laboratory and the machine room, offered a kind of hi-tech, medical-industrial doom, similar in some ways to the one they had visited upon the victims of the gas chambers.

Joseph Goebbels—the propaganda minister, made Reichskanzler in Hitler's last testament—and his wife Magda had already decided to kill their six children and then themselves. On April 27, Magda Goebbels had told SS doctor Helmut Kunz that she would have to kill her children and asked him to help. On May 1 Kunz was summoned and told that the time had come. They went up to the children's bedroom, where they were already in bed in their nightgowns. Magda handed the doctor a syringe filled with morphine and told the children they were getting a vaccination injection. Kunz injected the children so that they would fall asleep, but did not have the stomach to poison sleeping children, so Magda sent for Stumpfegger, and the two of them went from child to child putting an ampoule of poison between each one's teeth and forcing their jaws together to break each one. The presence of heavy bruising on the face of the eldest daughter Helga suggests that she may have struggled.

Afterwards Goebbels and his wife went up to the garden and crunched glass ampoules of cyanide between their teeth. They either shot themselves at the same time or had SS officers administer the *coup de grâce*. Their bodies were doused in petrol and burned. According to a Soviet autopsy report: "The remains of glass ampoules which had contained cyanide compound were found in the oral cavities [of Adolf and Eva Hitler]. These were identical to the ones found in the mouths of Goebbels and his wife."

Himmler and Goering

Apparently less keen on killing themselves were the two highest-ranking Nazis after Hitler, Heinrich Himmler, head of the SS and architect of the Final Solution, and Herman Goering, at one time the designated successor to Hitler. Both were taken prisoner by the Allies. Himmler had disguised himself and was equipped with false documents to conceal his true identity, but his papers were in suspiciously good order and he was arrested and recognized.

The following day, May 23, he was moved to a prison camp but before he could be interrogated he committed suicide by biting a cyanide capsule that he had hidden in his mouth. His last words were "I am Heinrich Himmler!" Doctors tried to administer emetics and struggled to resuscitate him, but after 12 minutes of death throes he expired—although a Jewish intelligence officer, Brigadier Susia Reich, who claims he was interrogating Himmler at the time and that the man died in his arms, described his death as "unfortunately quick and painless." His body was later buried in an unmarked grave.

An air of mystery and conspiracy has attended Himmler's death. And it has been suggested that the autopsy showed that his supposed corpse was missing identifying marks, and was that of a double. Others have suggested that he was murdered by the British to spare embarrassing revelations that they had been secretly negotiating with him. Conspiracy theories about him seemed to be supported by documents found in the British public records archive, but these proved to be forgeries, while proponents of the theories have included Holocaust deniers and Nazi sympathizers.

Mystery also attended Goering's suicide. He was captured and successfully brought to trial at Nuremberg, but decided to commit suicide when he was sentenced to death by hanging. On October 15, 1946, the night before he was due to be executed, he bit down on a cyanide ampoule he had somehow acquired and died despite efforts to resuscitate him. His body was nonetheless carried out to the scaffold to be shown to observers to confirm that he was dead. American reporter Kingsbury Smith described the scene: "As the blanket came off it revealed Goering clad in black silk pajamas with a blue jacket shirt over them, and this was soaking wet, apparently the result of efforts by prison doctors to revive him. The face of this twentieth-century freebooting political racketeer was still contorted with the pain of his last agonizing moments and his final gesture of defiance."

In 2005 a former U.S. soldier who had served as one of the guards during the Nuremberg trials, Herbert Lee Stivers, came forward to admit that he had unwittingly smuggled the fatal cyanide capsule to Goering. Trying to impress a pretty German girl, Stivers had agreed to pass to Goering fountain pens which he was told contained letters and medication, but which presumably contained cyanide ampoules—another was found among Goering's effects when his cell was searched. Whether Stivers's story is true is impossible to verify, but experts agree it is plausible.

Alan Turing

Alan Turing was an English mathematical genius credited with being the father of the computer, among many other achievements. On June 8, 1954, he was found dead in his bed, a half-eaten apple beside him. A later autopsy revealed that he had died from cyanide poisoning, and it is generally assumed that, overcome with depression after suffering appalling persecution for his homosexuality, he killed himself by injecting or painting one side of the apple with poison in a gesture laden with symbolism. But not everyone is convinced that his death was really suicide. Is it possible that Western security services murdered one of the most brilliant minds in their employ, a man whose genius and dedication had made him an unsung war hero?

The Lavender Scare

In 1954 Alan Turing was working at Manchester University as a research scientist, doing pioneering work on computers and also researching mathematical patterns in the natural world. Few of his friends knew that ten years earlier he had been a pivotal figure in the epic project at Bletchley Park to break the German Enigma code, work that would have made him a war hero if it had not been highly classified.

Instead he was now considered a severe security risk, thanks to what has been called, in a nod to the McCarthyite "red scare" of 1940s and '50s America, the "lavender scare"—a pathological fear among the higher echelons of the security services, especially in America, that homosexuality would prove to be the Achilles' heel of the West in the Cold War espionage battle. The military–security complex regarded many intellectuals as "pink" in two senses: both effete and worryingly liberal. More specifically, there was a general assumption that homosexuals could be lured with honey traps by Communist agents and then blackmailed—homosexuality being illegal at the time—to pass on secrets.

Incidents such as the defection of top British spies Guy Burgess and Donald Maclean, who were rumored to be gay lovers, had served to whip these fears into a frenzy.

Turing was considered a nightmare by security-conscious anti-communists. In addition to his involvement in the highly classified Enigma project, he had continued to be involved in high-level intelligence work related to codebreaking and computers. At the same time he was an open homosexual. In 1952 Turing had been burgled and he was certain that the culprit was an acquaintance of his gay lover. When he reported his suspicions to the police he had either naively or brazenly told them about his relationship, and they had promptly arrested him. Convicted of "gross indecency," he had been released from prison on the condition that he underwent hormone treatment with estrogen, a humiliating process that made him impotent and caused him to develop breasts and gain weight—a grave indignity for a keen long-distance runner. Turing also found himself barred from the U.S. and lost his security clearance, so that he was now denied access to much of the important work in which he had been engaged.

Now the object of great suspicion from the security services, he alarmed them still further by holidaying abroad in a search for gay sex. His destinations included countries worryingly near the Iron Curtain. Amid mounting anxiety about spies and homosexual honey traps, it is not implausible to imagine that Turing's assassination was at least considered.

The Poisoned Apple

In the two years following his conviction, Turing had become immersed in psychoanalysis. Intensive surveillance by the authorities caused him considerable stress, especially during one incident when he was suspected of involvement in the disappearance of a visiting Norwegian youth. His biographer Andrew Hodges describes his character at this time: "Eccentric, solitary, gloomy, vivacious, resigned, angry, eager—these were Turing's ever-mercurial characteristics, and despite his strength in defying outrageous fortune, no one could safely have predicted his future course." Whether these mood swings were sufficient to plunge him into suicidal depression is unclear, but on the morning

This c. 1860 illustration depicts Snow White drugged by a poisoned apple.
Obsessed with the Disney movie of the fairytale, Turing was fond of repeating the
witch's verse: "Dip the apple in the brew, Let the sleeping death seep through."

of June 8 his cleaner found him dead at his home in Wilmslow, Cheshire, a half-eaten apple by his bed. Always the scientist, he had various amateur chemistry equipment at home, including an apparatus for silver-coating spoons that included a tank of cyanide solution. This was the presumed source of the cyanide that killed him, and which he is generally believed to have applied to his apple before eating it—although the apple itself was not tested.

But why the apple? His mother, of whom he was very fond, suggested that he had got cyanide on his fingers from an experiment and accidentally ingested it along with the apple. But Hodges comments, "It is more credible that he had successfully contrived the manner of his death to allow her to believe this." Also, Turing was known to be an obsessive fan of the film *Snow White and the Seven Dwarfs*, and was fond of repeating the sinister verse of the witch: "Dip the apple in the brew, Let the sleeping death seep through." His choice of suicide by eating the poisoned half of an apple clearly seems to refer to the movie, suggesting a strange psychodrama involving fairytale archetypes, while the apple could even have been a reference to the forbidden fruit of the Garden of Eden, the apple from the Tree of Knowledge, in turn a reference to the carnal "knowledge" forbidden to Turing. It has also been suggested that he wished to echo scientific forebears such as Newton and Socrates, by coupling apples and suicide respectively.

Even now Turing's apple has endured in a strange afterlife of its own. Not only does it feature in a memorial sculpture of him in Manchester, in which he is seated on a bench holding an apple in one hand, but it is often credited with being the inspiration for the Apple Inc. logo, which shows an apple with a bite out of it. The latter is probably a myth, as the computer company's logo is a reference to Newton's apple, as evidenced by their short-lived original design which featured a picture of Newton beneath the apple tree.

Heaven's Gate

Marshall Applewhite was a music teacher from Texas who became the leader of a series of cults based on the belief that UFOs were spaceships piloted by aliens who were visiting Earth to bring enlightenment and help humanity reach higher levels of spiritual evolution. He and his partner Bonnie Nettles were known by various names, including Bo and Peep, and preached a strange mixture of Christianity and New-Age spiritualism.

Nettles died of cancer in 1985 but Applewhite continued to lead a small band of devoted followers, settling in California and calling themselves Heaven's Gate. Applewhite preached asceticism and celibacy, to the extent that he and six other male cultists had themselves surgically castrated. A core tenet of the cult was an extreme form of dualism: the belief that the soul and the body were separate entities. They believed that their current bodies were only temporary vessels and that at some point spaceships would arrive to carry their souls away to a new life.

Year of the Comet

That point seemed to have arrived with the appearance in the night sky of Comet Hale-Bopp in 1996. The brightest comet ever observed, it quickly aroused great excitement in the intertwined worlds of ufology and millenarian belief, particularly when an amateur astronomer claimed to have taken a photo showing a vast unidentified object, like a ringed planet, following in the comet's wake. "Remote viewer" Courtney Brown claimed to have clairvoyantly visited the object, ascertaining that it was a giant spaceship filled with aliens. Although these claims were subsequently demolished, the Heaven's Gate cult had heard enough to convince them that this was, in their own words, the "boarding pass" that would finally allow them to "graduate" to a "more than human" state.

PHENOBARBITAL

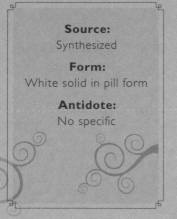

Source:
Synthesized

Form:
White solid in pill form

Antidote:
No specific

Overview Phenobarbital is a long-acting barbiturate with a variety of therapeutic uses, but which is highly dangerous in high doses. Barbiturates were first developed in the late nineteenth century for treating anxiety and insomnia. Phenobarbital, first made in 1904, proved to be a promising substitute for the bromides used to treat epilepsy patients, thanks to its long-lasting anticonvulsant properties. Like other barbiturates it also has sedative and hypnotic (sleep-inducing) properties. Also like other barbiturates, however, it has a low therapeutic index, which means that the difference between a therapeutic dose and a toxic dose is small. In the 1970s, before barbiturates became less widely available, they were the major drugs of choice for people committing suicide by overdose. Their potent CNS depressant effects seemed to offer a sure, painless, and peaceful route to oblivion.

Phenobarbital affects several organs, but its most important mechanism of action is in the CNS. The firing of a nerve cell depends on building up an electrical charge between the inside and outside of the cell—a process known as "polarization"—and this is accomplished by pumping ions in or out of the cell. Phenobarbital holds open the channels in the cell membranes that control the flow of chloride ions, and this causes hyperpolarization, which in turn suppresses the transmission of nerve signals, depressing CNS function.

Symptoms At low doses the suppression of neurotransmission causes therapeutic results, such as sedation, sleep, and anesthesia, but as the dose increases CNS depression progresses to coma—with such a marked decrease in the electrical activity of the brain that it resembles brain death—and eventually death due to respiratory arrest. Phenobarbital also affects the peripheral nervous system, causing paralysis, and the cardiovascular system. It can cause shock, sudden drop in blood pressure, and heart failure.

Treatment Phenobarbital is a "long-acting barbiturate," which means that it takes up to twelve hours to cross the blood–brain barrier, but also takes much longer to get flushed out of the system. There is no specific antidote, but supportive care is given to maintain breathing and heart function, and dialysis can be used to "scrub" the drug out of the blood.

FAMOUS CASES

Nazi Aktion T4
euthanasia program
(1939–41)

Heaven's Gate
mass suicide
(1997)

On March 21, 1997, all 39 members of the cult—21 women and 18 men, aged from 26 to 72—went to a restaurant for their last supper: 39 identical meals of chicken pie, salad, and cheesecake. The following day, back at the cult's large villa in Rancho Santa Fe near San Diego, they prepared for their final journey, packing overnight bags and dressing in identical outfits of sneakers, black shirts, and sweat pants, with armband patches bearing the legend "Heaven's Gate Away Team" in a strangely light-hearted nod to *Star Trek*.

Apple Sauce and Poison

To accomplish their "graduation" the cult chose the anti-epileptic drug phenobarbital (see left) as a way to ensure a relatively peaceful death. Having presumably crushed up tablets, they mixed it with apple sauce or pudding and washed it down with vodka, dispatching themselves in teams over three days, so that the whole process could be carried out in a neat and orderly fashion. Plastic bags were tied around the heads of each person after they had taken their fatal dose, and when they were dead the bags were removed and purple shrouds were placed over the bodies where they lay in their bunks. The last two cultists killed themselves on Monday, March 24, swallowing their poisoned sauce and placing plastic bags over their own heads. Videotaped farewell messages were sent to former cult members who alerted the police, and on Wednesday 26 a sheriff visited the house to be greeted with the stench of decomposition, but no signs of violence—unlike at Jonestown, the Heaven's Gate cultists had gone peacefully to their deaths, having chosen their poison well.

CHAPTER EIGHT

POISON

AS

SAVIOR

"In poison there is physic, and these news,

Having been well, that would have made me sick,

Being sick, have in some measure made me well."

Shakespeare (1564–1616), *Henry IV, Part II*

POISON IS A DOUBLE-EDGED SWORD, WITH THE POWER TO DO GREAT GOOD AS WELL AS HARM. AS THIS BOOK HAS REPEATEDLY SHOWN, POISON AND MEDICINE ARE TWO SIDES OF THE SAME COIN, BUT THE BENEFICIAL AND EVEN LIFE-SAVING APPLICATIONS OF POISONS EXTEND BEYOND PILLS. WITHOUT POISONS THERE WOULD BE NO ANESTHESIA OR CHEMOTHERAPY. OUTSIDE THE WORLD OF MEDICINE THERE WOULD BE SIGNIFICANT DEFICIENCIES IN FIELDS SUCH AS AGROCHEMICALS, INDUSTRIAL CHEMISTRY, AND ELECTRONICS. AND THROUGH SUCH APPLICATIONS, POISONS HAVE UNDOUBTEDLY SAVED MANY MORE LIVES IN THE LAST FEW CENTURIES THAN THEY EVER CLAIMED IN THE PRECEDING MILLENNIA.

This chapter explores some of these applications, looking at the debt that the modern medical chest owes to deadly toxins, and in particular at the way in which ancient poisons such as foxglove and arsenic were developed into clinical tools at the cutting edge of medicine. It explains the contribution made by poisons to the science of anesthesia—described by one of its pioneers, Horace Wells, as "the greatest discovery ever made"—from the mysterious medieval concoction "dwale" to the experimental new analgesics developed from cone-snail toxins. Finally it looks at how poisons have helped to transform agriculture and public health through the introduction of pesticides such as nicotine and organophosphates.

A drawing of the foxglove, *Digitalis purpurea*—from *Köhler's Medicinal Plants* (1887)—which for many centuries at least was an essential part of the herbalist's pharmacopoeia and a widespread folk remedy. It took science until the eighteenth century to catch up and turn it into a conventional medicine.

Physic from Poison

In his book *Poisons: From Hemlock to Botox to the Killer Bean of Calabar*, Peter Macinnis surveys the contents of the Squibb Pannier, the standard-issue medical chest issued to Union medics during the U.S. Civil War, which "reflected medical thinking in the 1860s, a time when medical knowledge was changing fast." Over half of the drugs in the Pannier, Macinnis points out, "are immediately identifiable as poisons." They included cantharides, tartar emetic, calomel (mercury chloride), tincture of opium, morphine, blue mass pills (mercury), aconite extract, and lead acetate, among many others. Many of these medicines dated back to Paracelsus, and even to ancient times (see chapter three).

Today the doctor's bag and the dispensing pharmacy are similarly stuffed with toxins, including a number that Civil War doctors and even Hippocrates and Galen might recognize, although some of them are now disguised by clinical names. Alongside these golden oldies are new ones developed by isolating, purifying, replicating, and modifying naturally occurring toxins. The whole field of pharmacology owes a massive debt to toxicology, to the extent that they are almost one and the same. Examples of killers turned healers include scopolamine, derived from belladonna and datura, and used as a sedative; atropine from the same sources, used as a sedative and anti-spasmodic; ergotamine from the ergot mold, used to treat bleeding; and botulinum from the botulinum bacteria, used to treat a range of disorders, from squint and cerebral palsy to excessive sweating and writer's cramp (all described elsewhere in this book).

The science of physiology also owes much to poisons. One of the main approaches to investigating biological processes is to interfere with them, and poisons are ideal for this. Their influence is sometimes reflected in the terminology derived from such research. For instance, two important classes of neuroreceptor are nicotinic and muscarinic, which derive their names from the role that the toxins nicotine and muscarine played in first isolating them.

Why Are Poisons Good for You?

The roll-call of therapeutic poisons poses a riddle: how can substances that are so bad for you be so good for you? The bottom line is that poisons can be deadly for the same reason they can be medically useful—because they are pharmacologically active; they are designed to interact with and alter molecules and processes in the body. The key for the doctor is to target these interactions and activities at cells, processes, and organisms that are deleterious to health, while avoiding as much as possible those that support good health. One way to do this is through controlling the dose of toxin that is administered, as discussed in chapter one. Another way is to limit exposure to the toxin to particular tissues and organs by direct targeting—for example, botulinum toxin is injected only into muscles or nerves that are causing problems, and the incidence of side effects depends to a great extent on the skill of the injecting doctor or surgeon. The ultimate expression of targeting came in Paul Ehrlich's attempts to turn arsenic into a "magic bullet" for killing disease organisms (see pp. 200–1). Exposure can also be limited in time; for example, 100 mg of atropine is normally a lethal dose, but given to a patient who has been exposed to sarin nerve gas such a dose could be a life-saver.

Magnified 16,000 times, these are *Clostridium botulinum* bacteria, the micro-organisms that produce probably the most potent toxin known. They are most famous as the source of a cosmetic treatment, Botox®, the commercial name for the toxin botulinum A, which blocks communication between nerves and muscles, effectively "silencing" the nerve. If injected into the right place this can produce therapeutic or cosmetic effects, for instance in the treatment of strabismus (crossed-eyes).

Hormesis Revisited

Recent research on the phenomenon of hormesis provides another possible explanation for the therapeutic effects of poisons. Hormesis, as touched upon in chapter one, is a dose-dependent phenomenon in which exposure to low levels of a toxin or other biologically damaging agent actually appears to stimulate health rather than damage it. Hormesis, from the Greek for "to excite," was first experimentally demonstrated in the 1880s in research on yeast, but since then it has been shown to operate in everything from bacteria to humans. Tiny doses of cadmium, for instance, boost the health of snails and butterflies, while low doses of radiation increase the lifespan of crickets and mice.

Hormesis works because it induces what is known as a stress response in organisms, in which defense and repair mechanisms swing into action. Once stimulated, these mechanisms go beyond simply repairing the low-level damage caused by the hormetic stressor; other damage or wear-and-tear is also repaired, and cell components may be strengthened or rejuvenated. For example, sirtuin 1 is a factor that is produced in response to mild stress; it activates genes that code for antioxidants and cell-membrane stabilizers. Another example, which could have relevance for recent research suggesting that nicotine (a powerful neurotoxin) is somehow protective against neurological conditions such as Alzheimer's, is the action of glutamate. Glutamate is a neurotransmitter, but is toxic to neurons at high doses. If glutamate release is triggered by a hormetic stressor, it in turn triggers neurons to release growth factors—substances that boost the survival and growth rate of these cells.

Perhaps some toxins achieve therapeutic effects through hormesis. If cells are exposed to levels that don't kill them outright, but simply stress them enough to trigger the release of stress factors, they will bounce back better than before. Literally, whatever does not kill you makes you stronger.

This phenomenon might have important consequences for the entire relationship between poisons and the public. If the hormesis model is correct, risk assessment of poisons will have to change—acceptable exposure levels might actually be higher than currently believed.

The Flower of Physic

A classic example of the transformation of poison into physic is the plant fox-glove, and its medical extract digitalis. Foxglove, *Digitalis purpurea*, is a striking plant distinctive for its bell-shaped flowers, rich in folkloric associations. The flowers are said to resemble the fingers of gloves, and this led to its original folk name, "folksglove"—a reference to the belief that flowers were worn by the fairy folk—which was then corrupted to "foxglove." A Scandinavian legend explains that the fox was given the blossoms by evil fairies, so as to soften his tread when he made raids on the farmer's chickens.

The active ingredients of foxglove are cardiac glycosides, potent toxins that affect the electrical properties of heart muscle. Such poisons have a long history of human use as arrow poisons, ordeal poisons, and medicine. The ancient Egyptians and Romans used a glycoside medicine called red squill, derived from the sea onion, as a diuretic, heart medicine, and rat poison. Digitalis had a variety of uses in folk and herbal medicine, although few of these related to its modern application. The sixteenth-century herbalist John Gerard, for instance, recommended it to those "who have fallen from high places," while another sixteenth-century herbalist suggested boiling foxglove in wine to produce an expectorant, although at the doses he recommended it was more likely to kill than cure.

The modern medical history of the digitalis preparation begins with the eighteenth-century physician William Withering, who became rich and successful practicing in Staffordshire, England. He was a keen botanist, and notable as the first man in Birmingham to own an indoor toilet. In 1775 he heard of a gypsy remedy for heart problems and tracked down the wise woman in question. Learning that the main ingredient of her medicine was digitalis, or extract of foxglove, he experimented systematically with various preparations and discovered a powerful new medicine for heart conditions, although it was over a century until its active ingredients were understood and became the medicines used today (see right). Withering's association with the foxglove prompted a cruel pun on the occasion of his final illness in 1799, when one of his friends observed that "The flower of physic is withering."

DIGITALIS

Source:

Foxglove (*Digitalis purpurea*)

Form:

Dried, powdered leaf; pure preparation: white crystalline powder

Antidote:

Atropine, digoxin antibody fragments (tradename Digibind)

Overview

Digitalis contains several cardiac glycosides (steroids with specific and powerful action on cardiac muscle), primarily digoxin and digitoxin, of which digoxin is the most medically important. They have what is known as a positive inotropic effect—they cause the heart to beat more slowly and regularly, but also more powerfully with each contraction. Unfortunately, the toxic dose for digitalis/digoxin medicines is close to the therapeutic dose, giving it a low therapeutic index. The result is that digitalis poisoning has been a severe problem ever since it was first introduced in the eighteenth century. In fact, the problem was worse then because the medicine was prepared from dried foxglove, making it very hard to control the exact levels of the active ingredients in each preparation. Withering specifically recommended that doctors proceed by giving miniscule doses and slowly building up to a therapeutic dose, but this was time-consuming. Now the glycosides are synthesized from scratch, so toxicity can be minutely controlled.

Today, those most at risk from digitalis poisoning are the elderly, who are often on long-term digitalis medication and can easily suffer problems because of interactions with other drugs. Between 10 and 18 percent of nursing-home patients develop digitalis toxicity. Other groups at risk are those on digitalis medication who also take herbal dietary supplements (natural liquorice, for instance, reacts badly with digitalis) and alternative medicines.

Symptoms

Digitalis poisoning can cause a variety of non-specific problems, such as dizziness, confusion, delirium, hallucinations, nausea, diarrhea, and blurred vision. More distinctive symptoms include disturbances of color vision that cause the sufferer to see yellows and greens, and it has been suggested that some of Van Gogh's vivid colorations, together with his mental instability, were down to digitalis poisoning. Most distinctive are cardiovascular problems such as palpitations, shortness of breath, blackouts, and irregular heartbeat.

Treatment

Atropine can be given as an emergency treatment, but the advent of Digibind, or digoxin antibodies, has radically improved treatment of poisoning. The antibodies mop up digoxin in the bloodstream.

FAMOUS CASES

Van Gogh
(1853–90)

EHRLICH'S MAGIC BULLET

A Nobel Prize winner for his ground-breaking work on the immune system, German medical researcher Paul Ehrlich could easily have won a second for his discovery of a cure for syphilis, a breakthrough he achieved by harnessing the lethal power of arsenic.

The Man with the Rainbow Fingers

Born in 1854 in Breslau, Germany—now Wrocław, Poland—Ehrlich trained as a doctor before moving into research, where in the course of his early career, he became proficient at using dyes. In fact, a teacher once pointed him out to a visiting scientist with the words, "That is 'little Ehrlich.' He is very good at staining, but he will never pass his examinations." Realizing that he could get dyes to stain specific targets—for instance, bacteria but not animal cells—he began to wonder if this useful property could be harnessed for medical purposes, searching for a dye that would not only stain disease-causing microbes but also attack them. His long hours of experimenting with different dyes meant he was notorious for his multicolored fingers.

Unfortunately, the infectious microbes got to Ehrlich before he got to them, for he contracted tuberculosis, possibly from micro-organisms in his laboratory. After two years recuperating in the hot, dry air of Egypt, he benefited from a new therapy called tuberculin—a kind of vaccination made from weakened TB bacteria—developed by Robert Koch, and went to work at Koch's institute. Here he plunged into research on "sera therapies"—treatments using the cell-free serum portion of blood, which was found to have potent immunological properties. He and his colleagues developed the concept of the anti-toxin, some sort of agent that was able to confer artificial immunity to animals injected with sera—now known to be antibodies, complex proteins produced by white blood cells.

The Search Continues

The sera research led to discovery of an antitoxin for diphtheria, which secured a Nobel Prize for Ehrlich's colleague von Behring, and in 1908 his own prize for his contributions to the theory of immunology. But Ehrlich was not satisfied, and remained intent upon his search for a "magic bullet," explaining:

> *"Picture an organism as infected by a certain species of bacterium, it will … be easy to effect a cure if substances have been discovered which have a specific affinity for these bacteria and act … on these alone … while they possess no affinity for the normal constituents of the body … such substances would then be … magic bullets."*

Continuing his research on specific dyes that might also be antibiotic, he and his co-worker, the Japanese bacteriologist Kiyoshi Shiga, synthesized a dye called trypan-red, which proved a useful treatment for sleeping sickness. Then, seeking an agent that would be even more toxic to its target cells, Ehrlich thought of arsenic. He and his co-workers synthesized hundreds of compounds of arsenic, and when they tested compound no. 606 on spirochetes—the micro-organisms responsible for syphilis—they struck gold.

Ehrlich's team had discovered a cure for syphilis, and it was released as Salvarsan, which along with its close derivative Neosalvarsan remained the most effective treatments for syphilis until the 1940s and the advent of penicillin-like antibiotics. Incredibly, however, there was considerable resistance to this cure, for syphilis was seen by many as a just punishment for licentiousness. In fact, Ehrlich was roundly abused for his degenerate researches. Then, when some patients died as a result of doctors not following Ehrlich's instructions, he was denounced as a fraud.

Exhausted by the attacks, Ehrlich suffered a series of strokes and died in 1915. Despite his successes he failed to realize his true dream of harnessing toxic molecules to antibodies. Even today researchers are still struggling to create the perfect drug delivery system that Ehrlich foresaw. He was a man ahead of his time.

THE MUSTARD GAS DISASTER

One of the most successful examples of the adaptation of poison for therapeutic ends has been the development of chemotherapy. Originally this meant simply the treatment of illness through the use of chemicals that kill cells, first demonstrated by Paul Ehrlich, the father of chemotherapy, with his organic arsenic compound Salvarsan (see p. 201). But in the more specific modern sense—the use of chemical agents to fight cancer—chemotherapy dates back to a terrible accident.

The Secret Disaster

On the night of December 2, 1943, the Italian port of Bari was crammed with Allied ships unloading munitions and supplies for the American armies fighting their way up the Italian peninsula. For some reason the air-raid warning system at the port failed and it was only when the bombs began falling that sailors and dockworkers realized the Germans had launched a raid. Seventeen Allied merchant ships were destroyed, one of them, the *Liberty*, blown out of the water as its cargo of high explosives detonated. Among the conventional weapons on board was an even more dangerous and shameful cargo—bombs loaded with mustard gas.

Mustard gas was a particularly unpleasant chemical weapon first employed by the Germans, and later by the Allies, in the First World War. An organic molecule with chlorine and either sulfur or nitrogen, it was a powerful vesicant (blistering agent) that incapacitated victims through horrible chemical burns that damaged the cornea, stripped the lining of the airways, and created huge blisters on exposed skin. Death was lingering and agonizing. Mustard gas—so named because the impure formulations used on the troops had a faint odor of mustard plants—also damages DNA through a reaction which mimics the effects of radiation, making it highly carcinogenic.

The raid on Bari, December 2, 1943. The Allies were caught unprepared as over 100 Luftwaffe bombers sank 17 ships in just over an hour, putting the harbor out of action for months and releasing deadly mustard gas in what was called by some "Little Pearl Harbor."

But why was an American ship loaded with this vile chemical weapon? The Allies claimed to possess such weapons for purely deterrent purposes, and indeed this ploy seems to have worked, for despite their many other atrocities the Nazis do not seem to have deployed any chemical weapons during the Second World War. Neither did the Allies, but they were sufficiently embarrassed about the presence of the mustard-gas bombs to designate the Bari incident "top secret" for 55 years.

It took a while for the authorities to realize what had happened, and by the time the poison-gas alarm was sounded hundreds of sailors and dockworkers had been exposed. Among the doctors treating the flood of casualties was the American physician Cornelius Packard Rhoads.

The Cancer Man

Like Ehrlich, Rhoads's interest in chemotherapy stemmed from his brush with tuberculosis, which he contracted as a young surgical intern. This had led him to an interest in pathology and immunology, and from these to cancers of the blood. He has been accused of taking part in experiments on unwitting human subjects, in particular of injecting cancer cells into a group of Puerto Ricans while researching there in the 1930s. It is even claimed that he wrote that the Puerto Rican population should be eradicated. After the Second World War he became involved in radiological research, and is further accused of carrying out unethical radiation experiments on soldiers, prisoners, and patients.

To the medical community, however, he was a respected figure even before he began to treat 600 victims of the mustard-gas disaster at Bari. Monitoring his patients, he noticed that their white blood-cell counts followed an intriguing pattern. After an initial rise in response to the toxic insult to the system, lymphocytes and other white blood cells began to disappear until there were none left, yet the patients' other tissues seemed unaffected. Eventually immature young white blood cells began to reappear in the patients' blood, showing that their immune systems were regenerating. Rhoads began to speculate on the possible use of mustard gas to treat leukemia, a cancer where white blood cells proliferate to dangerous levels. Perhaps mustard gas or a related agent could be a kind of "magic bullet," killing cancerous white blood cells without harming other tissues, so that new, healthy ones could replace them.

"Nitrogen Mustard"

The agent in question was "nitrogen mustard," and back in America doctors soon tried related compounds with immediate success. By 1945 Chicago doctor Leon Jacobson was able to report a sufferer of Hodgkins Disease in lasting remission thanks to nitrogen-mustard therapy. Rhoads went on to become a major proponent of chemotherapy, and the citation for a posthumous honor, the Katherine Berkin Judd Award, read: "It is safe to say that no one has contributed so much nor in so many ways to cancer research as did Dr. Rhoads."

Anesthesia and Analgesia

One of the most important advances in medicine has been the ability to induce anesthesia—the state of altered consciousness in which the sensation of pain is reduced or absent—and general anesthesia in particular. Before anesthesia, patients underwent excruciating agony during even the simplest surgery, and many died of shock. Complex surgery, such as gastrointestinal, cardiac, exploratory, or reconstructive surgery, was simply impossible. Anesthesia has spared untold suffering and saved countless lives, but amazingly the agents that have made it possible include some of the most notorious poisons. Even today the arms of the Association of Anaesthetists of Great Britain and Ireland features poppy heads alongside mandrake roots.

Sweet Dreams and Dead Sleep

The first man to use the term "anesthesia" seems to have been the Greco-Roman physician Dioscorides in the first century AD. It is Greek for "without sensation," and he used it in describing how a tincture of mandragora—extract of mandrake root, a member of the nightshade family—could be given to those "such as shall be cut, or cauterized... For they do not apprehend the pain because they are overborne with dead sleep."

Mandragora was mentioned again in the *Natural History* (c. AD 77) of Pliny the Elder, who writes that "For some persons the odor is quite sufficient to induce sleep." And later, the influential second-century Greek physician Galen—who spent four years as a doctor at a gladiatorial school—also recommended its use. The problem with all these ancient prescriptions is that mandragora has a very low therapeutic index: the dose needed to cause general anesthesia might well be lethal, and the patient might never wake up. This is one of the risks of using a poison as medicine. It may be that it was used more as an analgesic—a pain-relieving drug—than an anesthetic.

Opium was the other major agent of anesthesia in ancient times. Medical encyclopedist Aulus Cornelius Celsus, in his *De Medicina* of c. AD 30, wrote that opium juice "has been used to calm tempers and to induce pleasant dreams since the Trojan War and is still popular." But he warned that "Doctors should use it with circumspection… dreams can be sweet, but the sweeter they are, the rougher tends to be the awakening." A thousand years later the Persian physician and polymath Abu Ali al-Husain ibn Abdallah ibn Sina—known in the West as Avicenna—called opium "the most powerful of stupefacients." Both opium and the nightshades would go on to play major roles in the history of anesthesia to the present day.

Dwale to Make Men Sleep

Building on this ancient tradition, people in the Middle Ages could call upon a sophisticated arsenal of toxins turned lifesavers. In recent years a picture of medieval medicine has emerged that challenges the traditional view that anesthesia was first invented in the nineteenth century. Excavations at a hospital in Scotland have uncovered medical waste rich in evidence of drugs similar to today's pharmacopoeia; for instance, arsenic preparations used to treat lice and scabies, and opium mixed with lard used as an analgesic salve.

The most potent recipe from this period, however, was the concoction known as "dwale." Recipes for this anesthetic drink are known from at least 50 different sources in late medieval Britain, and a typical example reads:

> *"How to make a drink that men call dwale to make a man sleep while men cut him: Take three spoonfuls of the gall* [bile] *of a barrow swine* [boar] *for a man, and for a woman of a gilt* [sow], *three spoonfuls of hemlock juice, three spoonfuls of wild neep* [bryony], *three spoonfuls of lettuce, three spoonfuls of pape* [opium], *three spoonfuls of henbane, and three spoonfuls of eysyl* [vinegar], *and mix them all together and boil them a little and put them in a glass vessel well stopped and put thereof three spoonfuls into a potel* [4.75 pints] *of good wine and mix it well together."*

Although bile, bryony, vinegar, and lettuce are harmless, the other ingredients are highly toxic. In fact, the recipe reproduced above calls for lethal quantities, including ten times the fatal dose of opium or henbane, and as much as 35 times the lethal dose of hemlock juice. But it may be that the storage, handling, and boiling of the herbs dramatically lessened their toxicity, and it also seems unlikely that any patient would have drunk the whole "potel"—equivalent to three bottles of wine. Nonetheless, the variable toxic content of herbs means it would have been impossible for the toxicity of dwale to be controlled, and it must have been a high-risk remedy indeed.

The anthropomorphic root of the mandrake, *Mandragora officinarum*, with its concentration of psychoactive alkaloids has held great mystical significance.

The Heroic Remedy

The ingredient of dwale with the longest history of use is also the one that is most medically important today—opium. For most of history opium has been seen as a sort of miracle plant, "God's own medicine," in the words of influential Victorian physician Sir William Osler.

Opium was used in various forms, from poppy-tea to latex gum, but a more potable, effective, and easy-to-handle opium concoction was invented by Paracelsus (see p. 81), who proclaimed, "I possess a secret remedy which I call laudanum and which is superior to all other heroic remedies." His recipe included noxious additions such as frogspawn and crushed pearls, but most importantly it consisted of extract of opium in brandy, for the alkaloids are far more soluble in alcohol. Laudanum was later standardized by seventeenth-century physician Sir Thomas Sydenham—known as the father of English medicine—who mixed opium with wine, saffron, cinnamon, and cloves to create arguably the most important Western medicine until the late nineteenth century.

Eventually the influence of opium turned poisonous, as British gunboat diplomacy greatly increased its use in China and India, from where it fed back to the West. Meanwhile attempts to find purer formulations resulted in the isolation of morphine—wrongly believed to be non-addictive—and the introduction of the hypodermic syringe. Diacetylmorphine was synthesized in 1874 and marketed in 1898 as heroin—it was hoped that it would be more powerful and less addictive than morphine, but this proved only half true (see p. 19).

The key to the enduring popularity of opium has been its effectiveness at dulling both physical and psychological pain. Opiates remain among the most effective painkillers, and in the right context can be used safely.

Twilight Sleep

In the 1840s opiate and nightshade anesthetics were superseded by inhalants such as nitrous oxide, ether, and chloroform. Although nothing like as toxic as their herbal predecessors, these chemicals were dangerous nonetheless, because it was necessary to use concentrations that risked suffocating the patient, causing profound disturbances of metabolic function, or fatally depressing the cardiac function—ether was also highly explosive. And there were also contexts where they were not suitable for use.

In particular, the inhalants struggled to produce the complete muscle relaxation necessary for delicate operations. An important advance was the isolation of cocaine, from the coca plant of South America, in 1860. During the 1880s Sigmund Freud began researching it for use as a treatment for morphine addiction, and, noting its numbing effects, recommended it to Carl Koller, an ophthalmologist, who found it ideal for use in eye surgery. Although cocaine is no longer used for this purpose, derivatives such as novocaine are still employed, especially in dentistry and ear, nose, and throat surgery.

Another challenge was childbirth, in which rendering the laboring mother unconscious was impractical. One answer came in the form of "twilight sleep"—a mixture of morphine and hyoscine, or sometimes scopolamine, administered to ease the pain of childbirth without causing insensibility, while also causing the mother to forget her labors when she recovered. However, it could cause dangerous depression of the infant's central nervous system, and also found disfavor with mothers who felt alienated from their experience of childbirth. So it soon went out of fashion.

Snail Cures

Despite its major drawbacks, morphine is still widely regarded as the best analgesic—partly because there are few alternatives. However, among the most promising new drugs are conotoxins—potent poisons from cone snails. These are extremely specific in their action, and can be used to block targets, such as pain receptors, without affecting the rest of the system.

According to Dr. Bruce Livett of the University of Melbourne, one conotoxin being trialed for the treatment of neuropathic pain under the name Prialt "is between a thousand and 10,000 times more potent than morphine, but it is not habit forming, it's not addictive… [and] it doesn't cause respiratory depression." This is just one conotoxin, and with over 500 species of cone snail, they promise fertile ground for future research.

PESTICIDES

Corrosive sublimate, cyanide, arsenic, strychnine, and thallium are some of the most notorious poisons in history, yet their main incarnations have never been as tools of murder or suicide. The main reason for their manufacture was as pesticides, for it is against the animal kingdom that the killing power of poison has been mainly directed throughout human history. Through their use as pesticides, and particularly their role in controlling disease vectors such as malarial mosquitoes and typhus-bearing ticks, poisonous pesticides are arguably the greatest lifesavers in history. By controlling levels of agricultural pests, such as Colorado beetles and weevils, such pesticides have also helped ensure food security for billions of people.

Silent Springs versus Deadly Plagues

The use of toxic pesticides is, however, highly controversial, because although they are toxic to insects and other animals they are also toxic to humans. There is fierce debate over the relative merits of using such toxins as organochlorines and organophosphates—is it better to control dangerous and costly pests, or adopt a precautionary principle to protect the health of people and the environment?

The story of DDT is a classic illustration of this debate. Dichloro-diphenyl-trichloroethane is one of the organochlorines, a class of toxic chemicals that are much more dangerous to insects than to vertebrates. DDT works by opening channels in the membranes of neurons that control the flow of sodium ions. The channels become leaky, so that sodium ions pour out and the neuron becomes hyperexcitable and fires repetitively. The affected animal has spasms and eventually dies.

Although it was initially synthesized in 1874, it was not until 1939 that Swiss scientist Paul Müller discovered DDT's insecticide properties. It was immediately pressed into use during the Second World War to control pests that might spread diseases—mainly typhus and malaria—to the troops, and it was so successful that Müller was awarded the 1948 Nobel Prize in Physiology or Medicine. After the war DDT was used around the world to combat the malarial mosquito, with immense success. For instance, in Sri Lanka between 1934 and 1955 there were 1.5 million cases of malaria; after heavy use of DDT, 1963 saw just 17 reported cases. When the program was stopped in 1968 the number of annual cases jumped back up to around 600,000. In some other areas of the world malaria was effectively wiped out.

But this achievement had a cost. Organochlorines are persistent organic pollutants. They do not break down easily in the environment, and being lipid-soluble they tend to accumulate in the fatty tissues of animals and bioaccumulate as they move up the food chain, eventually building up to toxic levels in higher predators such as eagles and humans. Concern over the environmental impact of DDT led to the publication of Rachel Carson's seminal 1962 book *Silent Spring*, which swung public opinion against DDT and led to a massive decline in the use of organochloride pesticides.

Carson herself did not advocate that DDT should be completely banned from malaria-control programs, but this was largely the result.

The *Anopheles* mosquito, the vector for the parasite that causes malaria. Malaria is one of the world's most serious public-health problems, especially in the developing world. There are hundreds of millions of cases and up to three million deaths a year. Poison, in the form of insecticides such as DDT, has been a vital tool in the battle against malaria. In some parts of the world it has been credited with effectively eradicating the disease.

DDT is still used for indoor residual spraying, where small amounts are sprayed onto the walls of traditionally built houses in some parts of India and Africa, but even this is contentious. Some argue that it should be used on a much wider basis, others that it should not be used at all.

Nerve-Gassing Head Lice

The banning of organochlorides has led to an increase in the use of organophosphates—toxins related to the nerve gases. These have the advantage of breaking down quickly in the environment, so that they do not linger and bioaccumulate, which is better for wildlife and the consumers. But organophosphates are also hugely controversial because opponents argue that they are poisoning people who use or come into contact with them, and that they can be damaging even at levels far below the official safety limits. Organophosphate insecticides, such as parathion and malathion, are used in sheep-dips, for crop-spraying, against head lice, and for fumigating military equipment and even personnel. Opponents argue that they cause cumulative damage to peripheral and central nerves and the immune system, and may be linked to autoimmune diseases, neurological conditions, metabolic bone disease, cardiac diseases, Gulf War syndrome, chronic fatigue syndrome, and psychiatric problems.

Studies to look for these effects are contradictory and inconclusive, but opponents of organophosphates suggest that this is because the effects are subtle and involve interactions between toxins that are not properly understood. For instance, according to Dr. Goran Jamal, a consultant neurophysiologist at the Southern General Hospital, Glasgow, Scotland: "Exposure to very small doses could result in cumulative poisoning which may produce sub-clinical effects initially but render the individual susceptible to further toxic insults, thus producing progressive effects on the nervous system."

Such controversy over the roles of poisons in the world aptly sums up this chapter, and indeed this book. We have seen how poisons can kill or cure, how they can be used for good or ill, in circumstances by turns tragic or heroic, mundane or remarkable. And, to return to our introduction, it is this manifold nature that makes poisons, and the people who employ them, so fascinating.

NICOTINE

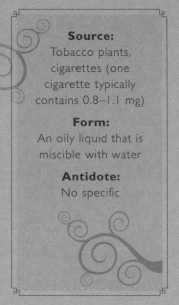

Source:
Tobacco plants,
cigarettes (one
cigarette typically
contains 0.8–1.1 mg)

Form:
An oily liquid that is
miscible with water

Antidote:
No specific

Overview Nicotine is familiar as the addictive ingredient in cigarettes, but few people realize that it is a highly potent alkaloid neurotoxin, which has been extensively used as an insecticide. The key to this dual nature is that nicotine exhibits a biphasic dose–response curve—it has one effect at low doses, and the opposite effect at high doses (it goes from being an agonist to an antagonist). Exposure to low doses normally occurs through smoking. In the past, most cases of acute poisoning occurred through contact with pesticides. Insecticide preparations can contain up to 95 percent nicotine. There have been cases of poisoning through skin contact with tobacco plants, and in one case a prisoner who had been picking tobacco in a plantation was poisoned when he tried to smuggle back into the prison tobacco leaves hidden in his rectum. Today, nicotine pesticides are rarely used in the developed world.

Symptoms Nicotine easily crosses into the bloodstream through the lungs (although when swallowed, stomach acid tends to interfere with absorption), reaching the brain within seven seconds. It quickly stimulates the release of neurotransmitters and hormones such as adrenaline and noradrenaline, increasing heart rate, respiration, blood glucose levels, and muscle contractions in the gut and bowel. It suppresses the appetite and stimulates the metabolism. By stimulating reward centers in the brain it can produce feelings of calm, alertness, and even euphoria, although the exact effects vary with the dose inhaled—small amounts cause an excitatory effect, while larger doses are depressive and therefore sedative.

Acute poisoning has very different effects. Death is most often caused by respiratory paralysis, which can occur very quickly with high doses, but if the victim survives long enough he or she may also experience torpor, giddiness, blurred vision and sensitivity to light, rapid and labored breathing, weakness and difficulty standing, relaxation of facial muscles, coldness, fainting, nausea, urgent need to pass urine, stool, and flatus, and eventually convulsions. High lethal doses usually kill within two hours.

Treatment There is no specific antidote for nicotine poisoning. Treatment must be supportive, to keep the heart and lungs going. Nicotine should be washed off skin and flushed out of the system. One suggested treatment is flushing the intestines with dilute peroxide to oxidize any residual nicotine. To counteract the CNS depressant effect, stimulants including coffee, brandy, atropine, and strychnine have all been tried.

Acknowledgments

For Michelle, the antidote to all ills.

p7 *Medea and Jason* (c. 1570–5) by Girolamo Macchietti © Alinari Archives | Corbis

p13 *Papaver somniferum* by Franz Eugen Köhler from *Köhler's Medicinal Plants* (1887) © Public domain

p15 Illustration of the poisoning scene from Racine's play *Britannicus* (1669) by Francois Chaveau © Gianni Dagli Orti | Corbis

p31 *Circe Pouring Poison into a Vase and Awaiting the Arrival of Ulysses* (c. 1850–98) by Edward Burne-Jones © The Gallery Collection | Corbis

p33 Coin depicting Mithridates the Great (c. 90 BCE) © Hulton Archive | Getty Images

p40 Venom on the Fang of a Diamondback Rattlesnake © Joe McDonald | Corbis

p43 Mexican Redknee Tarantula © Isselee | Dreamstime

p46 *Dinoflagellates Gymnodium* © Dr. David Phillips | Getty Images

p51 *Datura Stramonium* by Franz Eugen Köhler from *Köhler's Medicinal Plants* (1887) © Public domain

p54 Illustration of poisonous fungi from *Meyers Konversations-Lexikon Encyclopedia* (1897) © Bettmann | Corbis

p65 *A Mad Tea-Party* (1910) by M.L. Kirk © Blue Lantern Studio | Corbis

p74 *Hercules Vanquishing the Hydra of Lerne* (1620–1) by Guido Reni © The Art Archive | Musée du Louvre Paris | Alfredo Dagli Orti

p77 Roman Lead Piping from the reign of Marcus Aurelius (161–180 CE) © Vanni Archive | Corbis

p82 Engraved portrait of Paracelsus from his *Astronomica et Astrologica Pouscula* (1567) © Stapleton Collection | Corbis

p84 Arsenic © Lester V. Bergman | Corbis

p89 *Death of Chatterton* (1856) by Henry Wallis © The Art Archive | Tate Gallery London | Eileen Tweedy

p97 *The Death of Socrates* (1787) by Jacques-Louis David © Francis G. Mayer | CORBIS

p99 *Conium maculatum* by Franz Eugen Köhler from *Köhler's Medicinal Plants* (1887) © Public domain

p103 Erwin Rommel on October 1, 1944 © Hulton Archive | Getty Images

p107 Interior of Gas Death House of Nevada on May 24, 1926 © Bettmann | Corbis

p111 Canister of Zyklon B photographed on December 31, 1944 © Time & Life Pictures | Getty Images

p118 *Catherine de Medicis* (1585–6) by Santi di Tito © Arte & Immagini srl | Corbis

p123 Grigoriy Efimovich Rasputin photographed in 1916, the year of his assassination © The Art Archive | Musée des 2 Guerres Mondiales Paris | Gianni Dagli Orti

p131 *Ricinus communis* by Franz Eugen Köhler from *Köhler's Medicinal Plants* (1887) © Public domain

p135 (left) The platinum pellet that contained the ricin that killed Georgi Markov, photographed on September 30, 1978 © Hulton Archive | Getty Images

p135 (right) Georgi Markov © Handout | Reuters | Corbis

p138 Pitchblende rock © DK Limited | Corbis

p146 Illustration of Madame de Brinvilliers being tortured from an 1847 edition of *Crimes Celebres* by Alexandre Dumas © Stefano Bianchetti | Corbis

p155 Illustrations of Florence and James Maybrick from *The Graphic* (1869) © Public domain

p160 *Strychnos nux vomica* by Franz Eugen Köhler from *Köhler's Medicinal Plants* (1887) © Public domain

p163 Illustration of Hawley Crippen (1955) © Bettmann | Corbis

p167 Pyrite © Knorre | Dreamstime

p172 *Juliet Discovering Romeo's Body* (1890) by Ludovico Marchetti © Blue Lantern Studio | Corbis

p176 *Cleopatra Testing Poison on Condemned Prisoners* (1887) by Alexandre Cabanel © Christie's Images | Corbis

p178 Egyptian Cobra (*Naja haje*) © Dorling Kindersley | Getty Images

p180 Potassium ferrocyanide © Public domain

p185 The Seven Dwarves return to find Snow White unconscious after accepting the gift of a poisoned apple from a visiting crone (c. 1860) artist unkown © Hultan Archive | Getty Images

p194 *Digitalis purpurea* by Franz Eugen Köhler from *Köhler's Medicinal Plants* (1887) © Public domain

p196 *Clostridium botulinum* Bacteria x16,000 © Visuals Unlimited | Corbis

p203 Allied Ships Burning in Bari Harbour on December 2, 1943 © Bettmann | Corbis

p206 *Mandragora Foemina* (1610) by Basil Besler © Stapleton Collection | Corbis

p211 Light micrograph of an adult mosquito (Anopheles) © Visuals Unlimited | Corbis

GLOSSARY

Abortifacient An agent that causes abortions.

Acetylcholinesterase (AChE) An enzyme that breaks down the neurotransmitter acetylcholine.

Aconite A plant of the genus *Aconitum*, also known as wolfsbane.

Alchemy The medieval precursor of modern chemistry, especially involving attempts to turn base metals into gold.

Aflatoxin A toxic compound produced by *Aspergillus* molds.

Agonist An agent that binds strongly to neuroreceptors and stimulates them.

Alkaloids A class of pharmacologically active organic chemicals distinguished by the presence of carbon rings and a nitrogen atom.

Anesthesia A state of altered consciousness in which the sensation of pain is reduced or absent.

Analgesic A substance that relieves pain; or the property of relieving pain.

Anaphylaxis A state in which the immune system is hypersensitive to a substance and responds by triggering a systemic allergic response with severe and sometimes fatal consequences.

Antagonist An agent that interferes with the physiological action of neurotransmitters, especially by binding to and blocking their receptor molecules.

Anticholinergic The property of blocking the action of acetylcholine.

Antidote An agent that counteracts or interrupts the mechanism of a specific toxin.

Antioxidants Molecules that neutralize free radicals and prevent oxidative damage.

Antivenin An antidote consisting of antibodies to proteins contained in venoms.

Antivenom see Antivenin.

Apoptosis Orderly cell death. (See *also* Necrosis.)

Arousal In a physiological sense, the level of activity in the central nervous system, and thus alertness.

Arrhythmia An irregular heartbeat.

Arthropoda The phylum of invertebrate creatures with segmented bodies and exoskeletons; includes insects, spiders, and crustaceans.

ATP Adenosine triphosphate. A small molecule that provides the energy "currency" of the body's biochemical "economy."

Autonomic processes Those physiological processes not under conscious control.

Barbiturates Sedative drugs derived from barbituric acid.

Bezoar A stony concretion from the stomach of an animal, used to ward off poison.

Bioaccumulation The phenomenon whereby toxins build up in organisms as they ascend the food chain.

Bioavailability The extent to which a toxin can get from its source, for example, poisoned food, into the body.

Biomagnification see bioaccumulation.

Blood–brain barrier The interface between the blood and brain, which restricts the passage of solutes.

Calomel Salt of mercury, or mercury(I) chloride. A powder once used as a purgative.

Cantharides The poison made from the crushed cantharides beetle.

Carcinogen A substance that causes cancer.

Cardiac glycosides Toxic steroids that affect the electrical properties of heart muscle.

Ceruse An archaic term for white lead carbonate.

Chelating agents Chemicals that bind to metals and make them soluble.

Chemotherapy The use of chemical agents to fight cancer.

Cinnabar An ore of mercury.

CNS The central nervous system; the brain, brainstem, and spinal cord.

Congestive heart failure The condition in which the heart does not beat strongly enough and fluid collects in the lungs and other tissues.

Conotoxin One of a number of toxins from cone snails.

Contaminant Generally those substances that are toxic only at relatively high doses.

Corrosive sublimate An archaic term for salt of mercury, mercury (II) chloride.

Cyanide A class of chemical compounds in which an atom of carbon is joined to an atom of nitrogen by three bonds.

Cnidaria The phylum containing corals, sea anenomes, and jellyfish.

Cytoplasm The internal protoplasm of a cell.

Cytoskeleton The structure of the cell.

Detoxification The process of chemically altering toxic chemicals so that they become less toxic.

Digitalis An extract of foxglove, rich in cardiac glycosides including digoxin.

Dioxins A class of chemicals formed by burning hydrocarbons in the presence of chlorine.

Dose–response relationship The correlation between dose and response within either a group (quantal relationship) or individual (graded relationship).

Dwale An medieval anesthetic mixture of wine, opium, hemlock, and henbane.

Effective Dose The dose that takes effect within an organism. (See also External dose.)

Emetic An agent that causes vomiting, or "emesis."

Endorphins A class of signaling molecules involved in limiting pain and experiencing pleasure.

Enterotoxins Toxins that cause cell membranes in the gut walls to break down and leak fluids at very high rates.

Envenomation The injection of poison via a bite or sting.

Enzymes Complex biological molecules that catalyze reactions between other molecules.

Excretion The expulsion of waste, particularly the products of metabolism.

External dose The dose to which an individual is exposed (see also Effective dose).

Free radicals Indiscriminately reactive particles that will oxidize other molecules they come into contact with.

Fowler's solution One of a number of arsenical tonics prescribed for a range of illnesses.

Gastric lavage Artificial emesis via stomach pumping.

Gastrointestinal Relating to the stomach and intestines.

General anesthesia A state of unconsciousness during which the patient is unable to feel or experience anything.

Grain An archaic measure of weight, approximately equal to 0.065 g, 65 mg, or $\frac{1}{4400}$ oz.

Growth factors Substances that boost the survival and growth rate of cells.

Hallucinogen A drug that causes hallucinations.

Hellebores Poisonous plants of the genus Hellebores.

Homeostasis The maintenance of equilibrium within the body; in relation to toxins, the range of dosage with neither positive nor negative effects.

Hormesis The dose-dependent phenomenon in which exposure to low levels of a toxin is stimulating to health rather than damaging.

Hormetic stressor A stimulus, for example, a toxin, that triggers hormesis.

Hydropic degeneration The process in which cells soak up water, swell, and burst.

Hymenoptera An order of insects including bees, wasps, and ants.

Hyperkeratosis Abnormal thickening of the skin.

Hypoxia Oxygen deficiency in the tissues.

Inheritance powders see poudres de succession.

Inotropic Affecting the contraction of heart muscle.

Intravenous Into a vein.

Laudanum A tincture of opium in alcohol.

LD$_{50}$ Lethal Dose for 50 percent. The dose which is lethal for 50 percent of a population

Lipids Chemicals that are oily or fatty in nature.

Litharge A red lead oxide pigment.

"Magic bullet" A drug with lethal toxicity but which is totally specific for a pathogen.

Mandragora Extract of mandrake root, rich in scopolamine and atropine.

Metabolism The biochemical processes of the body.

Metabolites The intermediate forms in a metabolic pathway.

Mithridatum An ancient concoction with antidote powers, named for Mithridates the Great.

Mithridatic Of or relating to antidotes.

Mitochondria Cell organelles that produce ATP, the chemical source of a cell's energy.

Mustard gas A chemical weapon in the form of a volatile liquid, the gas of which causes irritation.

Mycotoxin Any toxin produced by a fungus.

Narcotic An addictive and usually illegal drug.

Necrosis The disorderly and uncontrolled death of cells. (See also Apoptosis.)

Nematocysts The specialized cells of some cnidaria that produce toxins.

Nerve gas Volatile chemical agents that vaporize easily and act as neurotoxins.

Neuron A nerve cell.

Neuropathy Dysfunction of peripheral nerves, as opposed to the CNS; for example, neuralgia

Neuroreceptors Molecules on the surfaces of neurons that neurotransmitters bind to in order to pass on nerve impulses.

Neurotoxin A toxin that targets neurons and synapses.

Neurotransmitter A molecule used for signaling between neurons.

Opium The drug derived from the opium poppy (*Papaver somniferum*).

Opiates A class of drugs derived from opium, or chemicals resembling these in structure and action.

Organelles Small functional bodies within cells.

Organochlorines A class of toxic chemicals that are much more dangerous to insects than to vertebrates; for example, dichloro-diphenyl-trichloro-roethane (DDT).

Organophosphates A class of toxic chemicals that includes nerve gases.

Orpiment A bright yellow arsenic sulfide ore formerly used as a pigment.

Oxidation The chemical process by which electrons are moved from one molecule to another; can damage cellular components.

Paracelsus Principle The principle that it is the dose that determines whether or not a substance is poisonous.

Parasympathetic system That part of the nervous system that inhibits the action of the heart and the stimulates the digestive system.

Pathogen A disease-causing agent; for example, a microbe.

Pharmacology The branch of medicine concerned with the use and effects of drugs.

Pharmacopoeia The range of medicinal drugs available or used within a society.

Piscicides Those poisons that are particularly toxic to fish, and are sometimes used for fishing.

Plumbism Lead poisoning.

Poison A substance that, when taken into or absorbed by living organisms, causes harm by means of its chemical action; especially a substance that is potent even in small doses.

Poisonous Containing poisons; or when differentiating from venomous, those animals with tissues that are partly or wholly toxic, but which have no means of actively delivering their toxins, except for being ingested.

Pollutant Generally those substances that are toxic only at relatively high doses.

Polypeptide A small protein molecule, or part of one.

Poudres de succession Arsenical poisons that were used to dispose of unwanted husbands or relatives. Also known as inheritance powders.

Proteolytic The property of breaking down proteins.

Prussic acid An archaic term for hydrocyanic acid (hydrogen cyanide in solution).

Psychotropic The property of affecting the mental state; similarly, psychoactive.

Purgative A medicine for emptying the bowels.

Realgar Red arsenic sulfide ore used as a pigment.

Respiratory system The collective term for the lungs and airways.

Sera therapies Those treatments that use the cell-free serum part of blood.

Solanaceous Relating to plants that are members of the nightshade family.

Spirochetes A phylum of bacteria, including those responsible for syphilis.

Steatosis The accumulation of lipids within a cell.

Stibnite Black antimony sulfide, an ore of antimony.

Stress response The cellular reaction to either a chemical or physical insult, in which defense and repair mechanisms are mobilized.

Subcutaneous Meaning under the skin, normally referring to an injection.

Synapse The gap between nerve cells, or between nerve and muscle cells, across which signaling molecules travel.

Synergy In a toxicological sense, where two toxins work together to produce an effect that is greater than the sum of the effects they would have independently.

Tartar emetic An archaic term for potassium antimony tartrate.

Therapeutic dose The dose at which a drug is effective in treating illness.

Therapeutic index The ratio of therapeutic dose to toxic dose; in other words, a measure of how safe a drug is.

Toadstone A fossil, reputedly from the forehead or stomach of a toad, with supposed powers to warn against poison.

Toadstool The common term for a toxic mushroom.

Tonguestone A fossilized shark's tooth, supposed to neutralize poisons.

Toxic dose The dose at which a drug starts to cause toxicity.

Toxic mechanism The way in which a poison produces toxic effects at a molecular and cellular level.

Toxication The process in which a chemical becomes toxic, or is made more toxic, through the metabolism of the body.

Toxicity The property of how toxic something is, and by extension the factors that determine how toxic it is.

Toxicologist One who studies the science of toxins.

Toxicology The science of toxins.

Toxin A specific toxic chemical with specific actions in the body.

Trypanosomes Single-celled organisms responsible for sleeping sickness and other diseases.

Twilight sleep A mixture of morphine and hyoscine, or sometimes scopolamine, administered to ease the pain of childbirth.

Umbelliferous Relating to or belonging to the same family of plants as carrots, fennel, and parsley.

Vacuole A tiny intracellular membranous bag.

Vasodilatory The property of causing blood vessels to widen.

Venom A cocktail of toxins in fluid, produced by an animal for active deployment.

Venomous As opposed to poisonous, an animal that actively deploys poison, delivering it by biting or stinging.

Vesicant A substance that causes blistering.

Volatile Changing from a liquid to a vapor easily.

White arsenic Arsenic trioxide.

Wolfsbane A folk name for aconite.

MEASUREMENTS

Because of the nature of poisons, this book follows the scientific convention of using metric units for most weights and volumes. Metric–Imperial conversions are as follows:

Weights

1 nanogram (ng) = 0.000000001 g ≈ $\frac{1}{2850000000}$ oz

1 milligram (mg) = 0.001 g ≈ $\frac{1}{28500}$ oz

1 gram (g) ≈ $\frac{1}{28}$ oz

1 kilogram (kg) = 1000 g ≈ 2⅕ lb

The archaic British measure of a grain is also referenced, and this is approximately equal to 0.065g or $\frac{1}{4400}$ oz.

REFERENCES

"Alkylating Agents: The Janus Effect," The Chemical Heritage Foundation, 2001; www.chemheritage.org/EducationalServices/pharm/chemo/readings/alkyl.htm

Bommakanti, Ananth S. and Waliyar Farid, "Importance of Aflatoxins in Human and Livestock Health"; http://www.aflatoxin.info/health.asp; accessed August 21, 2008

Arnett, Amy M., "Jimson Weed (*Datura stramonium*) Poisoning," *Clinical Toxicology Review*, Vol. 18, No. 3, December 1995

Barnett, Anthony, "Revealed: The Gas Chamber Horror of North Korea's Gulag," *The Observer*, February 1, 2004

Batty, David, "Q&A: Harold Shipman," *The Guardian*, August 25, 2005

Béarez, Philippe, "First Archaeological Indication of Fishing by Poison in a Sea Environment by the Engoroy Population at Salango (Manabí, Ecuador)," *Journal of Archaeological Science*, Vol. 25, No. 10, October 1998

Beevor, Antony, *Berlin: The Downfall, 1945*, Penguin, 2002

Bell, Gail, *The Poison Principle*, Picador, 2001

Bellamy, Patrick, "False Prophet: The Aum cult of terror," TruTV Crime Library; www.trutv.com/library/crime/terrorists_spies/terrorists/prophet/19.html; accessed June 2, 2008

Bowden, Mary Ellen, *Pharmaceutical Achievers*, Philadelphia: Chemical Heritage Foundation, 2003

Bradberry, S. M., Beer, S. T., and Vale, J. A., "Antimony," UK National Poisons Information Service, August 16, 1996; www.intox.org/databank/documents/chemical/antimony/ukpid40.htm

Brooks, Daniel E., "Plant Poisoning, Hemlock," eMedicine, June 19, 2006; www.emedicine.com/EMERG/topic875.htm

Capital Punishment UK; www.capitalpunishmentuk.org

Carter A.J., "Narcosis and Nightshade," *British Medical Journal*, Vol. 313, December 21–28, 1996

Carter, A.J., "Dwale: An Anaesthetic from Old England," *British Medical Journal*, Vol. 319, December 18–25, 1999

Casebook—Jack the Ripper; www.casebook.org

Centers for Disease Control and Prevention; www.cdc.gov

Clauss, James Joseph and Johnston, Sarah Iles, *Medea: Essays on Medea in Myth, Literature, Philosophy, and Art*, Princeton University Press, 1997

Coats, Joel R., "Mechanisms of Toxic Action and Structure-Activity Relationships for Organochlorine and Synthetic Pyrethroid Insecticides," *Environmental Health Perspectives*, Vol. 87, 1990

Connor, Steve, "Fossils: Myths, Mystery and Magic," *The Independent*, February 12, 2007

Cooper, M. R. and Johnson, A. W., *Poisonous Plants in Britain and Their Effects on Animals and Man*. HMSO, 1984

Cooper, Peter, "Poisoners and Politics," *The Pharmaceutical Journal*, Vol. 269, No. 7229, December 21–28, 2002

"Cornelius Packard Rhoads," *CA-A Cancer Journal for Clinicians*, Vol. 28, No. 5, September/October 1978

"The Crippen Case," *The Times*, September 27, 1910; http://archive.timesonline.co.uk/tol/viewArticle.arc?articleId=ARCHIVE-The_Times-1910-09-27-03-008&pageId=ARCHIVE-The_Times-1910-09-27-03

Crone, Hugh D., *Paracelsus, the Man who Defied Medicine: His Real Contribution to Medicine and Science*, Albarello Press, 2004

Cullen, Dr. Richard, "A Perversion of Justice: Exploding the Myth of Who Didn't Kill Rasputin," The Alexander Palace Time Machine; www.alexanderpalace.org/palace/Rasputinmurder.html; accessed July 17, 2008

Cutler, Robert W.P., *The Mysterious Death of Jane Stanford*, Stanford University Press, 2003 Emsley, John, *The Elements of Murder*, Oxford University Press, 2005

"The Death of Rasputin," *Time*, November 7, 1927; http://www.time.com/time/magazine/article/0,9171,731177,00.html

Death Penalty Information Center; www.deathpenaltyinfo.org

Discoveries in Medicine; www.discoveriesinmedicine.com

Dr. Bryan Grieg Fry's website; www.venomdoc.com

Drug Overdose; www.drug-overdose.com

eMedicine from WebMD; www.emedicine.com Encyclopaedia Romana; http://penelope.uchicago.edu/~grout/encyclopaedia_romana/index.html

England, Gerald, "Harold Fred Shipman: An Account of the Murderous GP of Hyde"; http://home.clara.net/nhi/shipman0.htm, September 22, 2005

Evans, Michael, "Spies with History as Poison Experts," *The Times*, November 24, 2006

"Evolution of Snake Venom Drew on Bits of Body Parts," UniNews Vol. 14, No. 5, April 4–18, 2005; uninews.unimelb.edu.au/news/2213/; accessed June 7, 2008

Farrell, Michael, *Poisons and Poisoners*, Robert Hale, 1992

Fischer, David W., "The Death Cap," American Mushrooms.com, March 7, 2006; http://americanmushrooms.com/deathcap.htm

Fletcher, Holly, "Aum Shinrikyo," Council on Foreign Relations website, May 28, 2008; www.cfr.org/publication/9238/; accessed June 3, 2008

Foldes F. F., "Anaesthesia Before and After Curare," Anaesthesiol Reanim Vol. 18, No. 5, 1993; www.ncbi.nlm.nih.gov/pubmed/8280340

"The Forced Suicide of Field Marshal Rommel, 1944," EyeWitness to History, 2002; www.eyewitnesstohistory.com

Foster, Patrick, "Dr Crippen May Have Been Innocent," The Times, October 17, 2007

Fox, Robin Lane, The Classical World, Allen Lane, 2005

Fry, Bryan G., Nicolas Vidal, et al, "Letter: Early Evolution of the Venom System in Lizards and Snakes," Nature Vol. 439, February 2, 2006

Fry, Bryan G., "Toxin Molecular Evolution," Venom Doc; http://www.kingsnake.com/toxinology/toxin_molecular_evolution.html; accessed June 15, 2008

Gardella, John, "The Cost-Effectiveness of Killing: An Overview of Nazi 'Euthanasia'," Medical Sentinel, Vol. 4, No. 4, July/August 1999

Gratzer, Walter, Eurekas and Euphorias: The Oxford Book of Scientific Anecdotes; Oxford University Press, 2002

Habal, Rania, "Barbiturate toxicity," eMedicine; www.emedicine.com/MED/topic207.htm; accessed September 5, 2008

Harding, Luke, "US pair fall ill in Moscow from thallium poisoning," The Guardian, March 7, 2007

Hermes, Matthew, Enough for One Lifetime: Wallace Carothers, Inventor of Nylon, Chemical Heritage Foundation, 1996

Hodges, Andrew, "Turing, Alan Mathison (1912–1954)," Oxford Dictionary of National Biography, Oxford University Press, 2004; www.oxforddnb.com/view/article/36578, accessed September 1, 2008

Hollington, Kris, How to Kill: The definitive history of the assassin, Arrow, 2008

Holt, Jim, "Code-Breaker: The Life and Death of Alan Turing," The New Yorker, February 6, 2006

Hornell, James, "Fishing Poisons," Man, Vol. 41, November/December 1941

Hudson, Christopher, "The French Führer: Genocidal Napoleon was as barbaric as Hitler, Historian Claims," Daily Mail, July 24, 2008

Iavicoli, S., Valentina Guastella, et al, "The Antimony Conflict," La Medicina del Lavoro, Vol. 1, 1997; http://lib.bioinfo.pl/pmid:17009674; accessed September 3, 2008

Infield, Glenn, Eva and Adolf, New English Library, 1976

"In Our Pages: 50 Years Ago: 1945: Himmler's Death," International Herald Tribune, July 3, 1995; www.iht.com/articles/1995/07/03/edold_0.php

Kiefer, David, "Du Pont Strikes Pay Dirt at Purity Hall," Today's Chemist At Work, Vol. 10, No. 4, April 2001

Kinnaird, Clark (ed.), It Happened in 1946, original edition 1947 reprinted in Carey, John (ed.) EyeWitness to History, Avon Books, 1987

Klaasen, Curtis D. and Watkins, John B. III, Casarett & Doull's Toxicology: Companion Handbook (fifth edition), McGraw Hill, 1999

Klaasen, Curtis D., Casarett & Doull's Toxicology: The Basic Science of Poisons, (seventh edition), McGraw Hill Medical, 2008

Kwon, Kenneth, "Digitalis Toxicity," eMedicine, July 14, 2006; www.emedicine.com/ped/topic590.htm

Lampe, K. F. and McCann, M. A., AMA Handbook of Poisonous and Injurious Plants, American Medical Association, 1985

Laurance, Jeremy, "Prozac, Opium, and Myrrh: The Ancient Arts of Anaesthesia are Unlocked," Independent, September 12, 1997

Leavitt, David, The Man Who Knew Too Much: Alan Turing and the Invention of the Computer, Phoenix, 2007

Levey, Martin, Early Arabic Pharmacology, E. J. Brill, 1973

Levy, Joel, Secret History, Vision, 2004

Levy, Joel, The Little Book of Conspiracies, Portobello Books, 2006

Lewis, Leo, "Japan Gripped by Suicide Epidemic," The Times, June 19, 2008

Lifton R., The Nazi Doctors, Basic Books, 1986

Livett, Bruce, "Coneshell and Conotoxin homepage,"August 10, 2005; grimwade.

biochem.unimelb.edu.au/cone/applicat.html

López, T. A., Cid, M. S., and Bianchini, M. L., "Biochemistry of Hemlock (Conium maculatum L.) Alkaloids and Their Acute and Chronic Toxicity in Livestock. A review," Toxicon, Vol. 37, No. 6, June 1999

Macinnis, Peter, The Killer Bean of Calabar and Other Stories, Allen & Unwin, 2004

Mackay, Charles, Extraordinary Popular Delusions and the Madness of Crowds, first published 1841, this edition Wordsworth Reference, 1995

Mann, John, Life Saving Drugs: The Elusive Magic Bullet, Royal Society of Chemistry, 2004

Mattson, Matthews and Calabrese, Edward, "Best in small doses," New Scientist, August 9, 2008

May, Paul, "Digitalis," Molecule of the Month, 1996; www.bristol.ac.uk/Depts/Chemistry/MOTM/digitalis/digtalis.htm

Missen, Dr. Chris, "Behind the Mask," BBC Online, January 31, 2000; http://news.bbc.co.uk/1/hi/in_depth/uk/2000/the_shipman_murders/the_shipman_files/607002.stm

"Mites are the Primary Source of Poison Arrow Frog Toxins," mongabay.com, May 14, 2007; http://news.mongabay.com/2007/0514-frogs.html

Moore, Rebecca, In Defense of Peoples Temple-And Other Essays, Edwin Mellen Press, 1988

Newman, Cathy, "Pick Your Poison – Twelve toxic tales," National Geographic, May 2005

"Nicotine Drug 'May Slow Dementia'," BBC News, July 13, 2008; http://news.bbc.co.uk/go/pr/fr/-/1/hi/health/7497037.stm

Olson, Kyle, "Aum Shinrikyo: Once and Future Threat?" Emerging Infectious Diseases, Vol. 5, No. 4, July/August 1999

Pearce, David, "The Plant of Joy," 1999; http://opiates.net/

Pearce, David, "Utopian Surgery," Discoveries in Medicine, 2008; www.general-anaesthesia.com/#historical

Pesticide Action Network UK, "Organophosphate Insecticides"; Pesticides News No. 34, December 1996

Podolsky, M. Lawrence and Podolsky, Daniel K., *Cures Out of Chaos: How Unexpected Discoveries Led to Breakthroughs in Medicine and Health*, CRC Press, 1997

Pool, Bob, "Former GI Claims Role in Goering's Death," *LA Times*, February 7, 2005

"Precious Stones Guide: Vol. 11"; www.jjkent.com/articles/precious-stones-guide-vol11/index.htm; accessed June 3, 2008

Proudfoot, Alex, "The Early Toxicology of Physostigmine: A Tale of Beans, Great Men and Egos," *Toxicological Review*, Vol. 25, No. 2, 2006

Pueschel, Matt, "Claudius Likely Victim of Poisonous Mushroom," *U.S. Medicine*, March 2001

Ramsland, Katherine, "The Heaven's Gate Cult," Crime Library, www.trutv.com/library/crime/notorious_murders/mass/heavens_gate/5.html; accessed August 23, 2008

Reigart, J. Routt and Roberts, James R., "Recognition and Management of Pesticide Poisonings," EPA Office of Pesticide Programs, 1999; www.epa.gov/pesticides/safety/healthcare

Roberts, Margaret F. and Wink, Michael: *Alkaloids: Biochemistry, Ecology, and Medicinal Applications*, Springer, 1998

Sharav, Vera Hassner, "Human Experiments: A Chronology of Human Research," Alliance for Human Research Protection; www.ahrp.org/history/chronology.php

Shea, Dana and Gottron, Frank, "Ricin: Technical Background and Potential Role in Terrorism," CRS Report for Congress, February 4, 2004; www.iwar.org.uk/cyberterror/resources/crs/ricin.pdf

Sixsmith, Martin, *The Litvinenko File*, Macmillian, 2007

Somerset, Anne, *The Affair of the Poisons: Murder, Infanticide, and Satanism at the Court of Louis XIV*, St Martin's Press, 2004

Sreenivasan, Aparna, "Keeping Up With the Cones," *Natural History*, Vol. 111, No.1, February 2002

Stevens, Serita and Bannon, Anne, *Book of Poisons: A Guide for Writers*, Writer's Digest Books, 2007

Stone, Trevor and Darlington, Gail, *Pills, Potions and Poisons*, Oxford University Press, 2000

"The story of Mary Ann Cotton: A Frail Dressmaker's Poisonous Past," *Watford Observer*, September 20, 2007; www.watfordobserver.co.uk/news/263745.the_story_of_mary_ann_cotton_a_frail_dressmakers_poisonous_past/

Thompson, C. J. S., *Poison Mysteries in History, Romance and Crime*, first published 1923, this edition Kessinger Publishing, 2003

Thompson, Damian, *The End of Time: Faith and Fear in the Shadow of the Millennium*, University Press of New England, 1997

Timbrell, John, *The Poison Paradox*, Oxford University Press, 2008

"Toxicological Profile for Cyanide," Agency for Toxic Substances and Disease Registry, 2006; http://www.atsdr.cdc.gov/toxprofiles/tp8-c3.pdf

Toxipedia, www.toxipedia.org

Tyldesley, Joyce, "Cleopatra: Last Queen of Egypt," *Profile*, 2008

Vankin, Jonathan and Whalen, John, *The 80 Greatest Conspiracies of All Time*, Citadel Press, 2004

Vaults of Erowid, online library on psychoactive drugs, plants, and chemicals; www.erowid.org

"Viktor Yushchenko Points Finger at Russia Over Poison That Scarred Him," *The Times*, September 11, 2007

Volodarsky, Boris, "The KGB's Poison Factory," *Wall Street Journal*, April 7, 2005

Walsh, Nick Paton, "Markov's Umbrella Assassin Revealed," *The Guardian*, June 6, 2005

Waring, R. H., Stevenson, G. B., and Mitchell S. C. (eds), *Molecules of Death* (second edition), Imperial College Press, 2007

Wessinger, Catherine, *How the Millennium Comes Violently: From Jonestown to Heaven's Gate*, Seven Bridges Press, 2000

White, Michael, *Isaac Newton: The Last Sorcerer*, Fourth Estate, 1998

Wolf, Paul, M. D., "The Effects of Diseases, Drugs, and Chemicals on the Creativity and Productivity of Famous Sculptors, Classic Painters, Classic Music Composers and Authors," *Archives of Pathology and Laboratory Medicine*, Vol. 129, No.11, 1995

Wolfe, Susan, "Who Killed Jane Stanford?" *Stanford Magazine*, September/October 2003

Wright, Stephen and Williams, David, "Revealed: Poisoned ex-Russian Spy Litvinenko was a Paid-Up MI6 Agent," *Daily Mail*, October 27, 2007

Zimmers T. A., Sheldon J., et al, "Lethal Injection for Execution: Chemical Asphyxiation?" *PLoS Med* Vol. 4, No. 4, 2007; e156 doi:10.1371/journal.pmed.0040156

INDEX

aconite 70, 71, 73, 195

Agrippina 85, 117–19

alchemists 62–4, 153

antimony 59–60, 71, 153, 165–6
  see also Chapman, George; tartar emetic

Aqua Toffana 80, 85

arrow poisons 70, 73–5

arsenic 80, 84–9, 144, 145, 210
  as medicine 27, 59, 60, 196, 200–1, 207 (see also Fowler's Solution)
  soap 145, 147
  tests for 83
  white arsenic 83, 84, 85, 86, 88, 121
  see also Cotton, Mary Ann; Maybrick, Florence; realgar

atropine 25, 52, 95, 165, 195, 196

Augustus (Octavian) 77, 116–17, 175–6, 178

bees 44

belladonna 52, 71, 117

Bennett, John Hughes 100

Berezovsky, Boris 136, 139

bezoars 30

Bleyer, J. Mount 105

blue pills 59

Borgias, the 78–9, 119

botulinum 49, 195, 196

Brinvilliers, Madame de 80, 144, 146

Britannicus 15, 117–18

cadmium 29, 197

Calabar beans 94, 95, 105

Cantarella, La 78–9, 85

cantharides 45

Carr, Robert 120–2

cassava 28–9

castor beans 28, 50

castor oil 102

Cellini, Benvenuto 29

Celsus, Aulus Cornelius 206

Chambre Ardente 144–5

Chapman, George (Severin Klosowski) 150–2

Charles II, of England 63–4

Chatterton, Thomas 89

chemotherapy 202, 204

cholera 48

Christison, Robert 105

cinnabar 63

Circe 30, 31

Claudius 117

Cleopatra 80, 175–8

cocaine 209

Commodus 119

cone snails 47, 209

corrosive sublimate 29, 121–2, 144, 210

Cotton, Mary Ann 147–9

coup de poudre 47

Crippen, Dr. Hawley Harvey 161–4

cyanide 20, 124–5, 126, 128, 166, 183, 186, 210
  hydrogen cyanide gas 106–7, 110

suicide pills 104, 126, 180–2

Cyclon B see Zyklon B

Darwin, Charles 87

Datura stramonium 51–3

DDT 210–12

death cap mushrooms 54, 57, 117

Demosthenes 172–4

Digitalis purpurea 71, 194, 198–9

Dioscorides 31, 73, 205

Domitian 119

dose–response relationship 26–9

dwale 207

Ehrlich, Paul 196, 200–1, 202

electric chair, the 105, 107

Elwes, Sir Gervase 121–2

emetics 31, 32

ergot 58, 195

fly agaric 54, 55, 117

Ford, Arthur 45

Fowler's Solution 85–7, 155

Freud, Sigmund 209

frogs 44, 70

fugu, the 47

funnel-web spiders 28, 43

gas chambers
  Nazi 109, 110–11
  North Korean 111
  U.S. executions 106–7

gas vans, Nazi 109–10

gastric lavage 31–2
Goebbels, Joseph 181
Goering, Herman 181, 182
Gosio, Bartolomeo 87
Greece, ancient 72–5
  see also Demosthenes;
    Socrates
Gulf War syndrome 25, 212
Gullino, Grancesco 134–5

Heaven's Gate suicides 187–9
hemlock 71, 99–100, 101, 207
Hercules 73–5
heroin 13, 19, 32–3, 208
Himmler, Heinrich 179, 181–2
Hitler, Adolf 102, 103, 104,
  179–80
hormesis 27, 197
Howard, Frances 120–2
Hussein, Saddam 85, 128
hyoscine see scopolamine

injections, lethal 107–8
inland taipan 40–1

Jacobson, Leon 204
James's Powder 60
Jamestown poisonings 51–3
Jean of Navarre 80
jellyfish 46–7
Jordan, David Starr 157, 159–60

Kamera 127, 128, 134, 139
Khokhlov, Nikolay 128
Klosowski, Severin see Chapman,
  George

laudanum 208
la Voisin (Catherine Deshayes)
  45, 80, 144–5
lead 59, 60, 71, 75–7
LeFarge, Madame 83

lewisite 85
Liquor Epispasticus 45
Litvinenko, Alexander 128,
  136–9
Livia Augusta 116–17
Locusta 117–19
Luce, Clare Boothe 87
Lugovoi, Andrei 138, 139

Maimonides, Moses 81
Mairanovsky, Grigory 127
malaria 211
mandrake, the 51, 205, 206
Markov, Georgi 129–35
Marsh, James 82–3
Maybrick, Florence 154–6
Medici, Catherine de 80, 118,
  119
mercury 16, 20, 28, 38, 59, 60–5
  see also corrosive sublimate
metabolism 17–18
Minamata Bay poisonings 62
Mithridates the Great 33
molds 56
  see also ergot
Montecuccoli, Sébastien 119
Montespan, Marquise de 145
morphine 13, 19, 105, 195,
  208, 209
muavi 94
mushrooms 54–6, 57, 117
mussels 46
mustard gas 127, 202–5

naloxone 32–3
Napoleon I 87, 97, 109
Nero 117–19
Newton, Isaac 63, 153
Nicander of Colophon
  72, 76, 100
nicotine 195, 197, 213

Octavian see Augustus
octopus, blue-ringed 47
Odysseus 30, 70
Okolovich, Georgy 128
opium 13, 71, 100, 195, 206,
  207, 208
ordeal, trials by 94–5
Ordeal Beans of Calabar 94,
  95, 105
Orfila, Mathieu 83
organochlorides 210–12
organophosphates 210, 212
orpiment 85, 87
Overbury, Thomas 120–2

Paracelsus 60, 81, 208
Paracelsus Principle 26
Parysatis 116
peanuts 56
perpetual pills 59–60
pesticides 210–13
phenobarbital 188, 189
phossy jaw 62
piscicides 71
plants, toxicity of 50–1
pokeweed 51
polonium-210 137–8
poudres de succession 80, 85
Prialt 209
Putin, Vladimir 127, 136

Rasputin, Grigory Efimovich
  123–5
ratsnakes 39
Rayner, Oswald 125
realgar 85, 87, 121
Rebet, Lev 128
Rene the Florentine 80
Rhoads, Cornelius Packard
  203–4
ricin 20, 28, 50, 71, 131, 133
  see also Markov, Georgi

Romans, ancient 72, 75–7, 84, 116–19
Romeo 173
Rommel, Erwin 102–4

Sade, Marquis de 45
sapa 77
sarin 22, 23, 25
sassy bark 94
Scaramella, Mario 138, 139
Scheele, Karl 87
scopolamine 52, 53, 162, 164, 195, 209
scorpions 44, 71
Shen Nung 71
snakes 33, 39, 40–1, 42, 70, 71
    see also Cleopatra
sneeze gas 85
Socrates 96–100
Spanish fly 45

Spara, Hieronyma 79
spiders 42–3
Stanford, Jane 157
stibnite 59
Stivers, Herbert Lee 182
strychnine 51, 158, 160, 210
    see also Stanford, Jane
Styrians/Styrian Defense 87–8, 89, 156
Susruta 71
Sydenham, Sir Thomas 208

tarantulas 43
tartar emetic 60, 151, 153, 195
tests for poisons 82–3
tetrodotoxin 47
thallium 165, 166–7, 210
Thrasyas of Mantineia 100, 105
ticks 44
toads 44, 80

toadstone 30–1
toadstools 55–6
Tokyo Subway attacks 21–3
tonguestones 31
Tophania of Naples 80
trials by ordeal 94–5
Tsepov, Roman 137
Turing, Alan 183–6
"twilight sleep" 208–9

water 26
Wetterhahn, Karen 16
Withering, William 198, 199

Young, Graham 165–7

Zhivkov, Todor 129, 134
zombies 47
Zyklon B 110–11